Photo by Ron Bailey

Over the Hill

Graham Wilson

OVER THE HILL

A string of mountain matters

Millrace

First published in Great Britain in 2011 by
Millrace
2a Leafield Road, Disley
Cheshire SK12 2JF
www.millracebooks.co.uk

ISBN: 978-1-902173-337

Typeset in Adobe Garamond Pro.
Printed and bound in the United Kingdom
by T J International Ltd, Padstow, Cornwall PL28 8RW

Under the hill: the author in 1965
Photo by Patricia Wilson

Acknowledgements

I would especially like to acknowledge the work of those editors and contributors who have made possible the Journals of the Fell and Rock Climbing Club, the Climbers' Club and the Rucksack Club. Not only for the information I have mined from this treasury, but also for the overall contribution they have made, and continue to make, to the history and literature of climbing in this country.

In a similar vein, I would like to acknowledge Canongate Books (*High Endeavours*, Jimmy Cruickshank), J M Dent & Sons (*Undiscovered Scotland*, W H Murray), Victor Gollancz (*On and Off the Rocks*, Jim Perrin, and *One Man's Mountains*, Tom Patey), Rupert Hart-Davis (*Gervasutti's Climbs*, Giusto Gervasutti) and Secker & Warburg (*Climbing Days*, Dorothy Pilley). In particular I would like to thank both Ernest Press (*Creagh Dhu Climber*, Jeff Connor) and Ken Wilson (first with Diadem (*Undiscovered Scotland*) and later Baton Wicks) who have done so much to keep the tradition alive. Details of all quoted publications are to be found in the Notes at the end of the book.

I would also like to thank Robin Hidden for the jacket illustration, Joy Parsons for permission to use her late husband's photograph on the endpapers of the special edition, and Dr Elizabeth Cripps for her lucid explanation of the principles of Environmental Philosophy.

Contents

The One that Got Away

Seek and ye shall find! This enthusiastic exhortation tends to lose its edge as life passes you by. But, in youth, there is no doubt: the Quest's the Thing. My own attempt at self-enlightenment had two strands, separate but not necessarily unconnected. This combination of grails was to discover, first, a lump of virgin rock where I could chart routes of character—the names of which would ring through climbing history as did Eagle's Nest Direct, Longland's Climb and Cenotaph Corner—and, second, a public house that served late.

To modern ears, the latter must sound singularly unambitious but in those forgotten days of 'You've never had it so good', one benefit that missed the package of general well-being was the public opportunity to consume, or even be in possession of, alcohol after ten o'clock. There was no leeway. Cometh the hour, so early that any self-respecting witch would still have been snuggled under the duvet, cometh the bell. Grills were slammed on grasping fingers, chairs were piled around those who had the temerity to remained seated and the valedictory drone of the vacuum cleaner bid the hesitant its sonorous farewell.

Everyone *knew* someone who had met someone who had once spoken to an imbibing Marco Polo who had roistered away the small hours in a valhalla where a pint of Fed passed for nectar, but no one could supply as much as a one-figure map reference. So, as with the mystical Jug & Bottle skulking in some half-lit back alley, tales abounded in my youth of an elusive Mystery Buttress. But all reported trails seemed to end at some scattered lumps of tot, covered with sheep, or, if a steep unbroken face, more suitable for pole-vaulting than self-promoting feats of callisthenics.

Yet it was no fool's errand. History, at least, was on my side, recording that a Mystery Buttress had existed and, moreover, was of such size and shape that it would have more than held its own in the classic playgrounds of the gritstone pioneers. It lay on an uninhabited stretch of moorland between Burnley and Hebden Bridge. No road and scarcely a track ran across this wasteland, the centre of which was separated from public transport by five or six miles in any direction. So, not surprisingly, unlike the Peak District or the moors that rise above the chimneys and mills of industrial Yorkshire, the area was little visited. All that distinguished it from the land so cherished by Catherine and Heathcliff was a reservoir built towards the end of the nineteenth century and, above these waters, a looming lump of rock.

Although Maurice Linnell hit upon the buttress in 1926, three years elapsed before H K Hartley rediscovered the crag. No doubt whispers hung in the air but Hartley managed to keep the location secret, hoping to clean up before others arrived. The outcome must have exceeded his expectations. In addition to Linnell's original, he found four other routes, each, by the standards of its day, with distinctive merits of its own. What many of the founding fathers wanted were routes that offered a microcosm of the greater crags, to wit a series of rock pitches separated by secure stances, and Widdop Buttress clearly filled the bill.

Hartley's Ordinary Route was anything but. In the course of its 100 feet, pitches abound (originally five), with a variety of cracks and walls linked by a stomach traverse. His follow-up, The Three Cs, was an excursion in triplicate, which faithfully followed tradition by awarding proper names to various high points of difficulty. Anyone approaching the Caterpillar (a wriggle), Cascara (a purgative), and the Corbel (an awkward architectural feature) was duly forewarned. The Victorian stray had been roped in.

Yet if Hartley's find was unusual, then those of T Graham Brown were all the more remarkable. Not only did he discover a new crag with climbs in excess of 200 feet but one at the very epicentre of Lake District climbing. The chance of coming across an unknown cliff at such a late stage of rock-climbing history seemed virtually impossible. Particularly as it contained little in the way of the nasty-looking overhangs and frictionless slabs that lay beyond the relatively primitive technique and equipment of the time. Brown's eight first ascents provided over 1,500 feet of climbing graded from Diff to Middlish Severe, which, between the wars, would have only been regarded as testing for the averagely good climber rather than the expert.

This neglected crag lay on the north face of Kirk Fell, less than two miles from the front door of the Wasdale Head Hotel and a few hundred yards from Moses Trod and the Gable Traverse. Brown first saw these rocks in 1912 when, as a newcomer to the district, he was tramping the fells trying to catch his bearings. His searches had taken him along a path, probably no more than a sheep trod, that ran across the northern flank of fell separating Beckhead from Black Sail. It was during this high-level traverse that he noticed a series of cliffs and, in particular, a fine soaring central pillar, the full significance of which no doubt eluded him at the time but which later he was to describe for the Fell and Rock Journal as the 'cleanest and finest piece of isolated rock in the Lake District!'[1]

A year or so later, after he had been introduced to the pleasures of rock climbing proper but before he had time to retrace his memories, the War intervened. During those dark and difficult years, he recalled that his spirits were sustained by thoughts of what he might discover when the conflict was over. But by the time he was discharged from the army, he was still in a pretty bad way and a number of years elapsed before he had sufficiently recovered to attempt any proper climbing. By then, he was certain that, if reality had matched up to his imagination, the crag would have been discovered and mentioned in despatches. As a result, he felt it tactless to persuade others to waste a day of their precious holiday on what might well be a wild-goose chase.

So it was not until the last day of 1924, when walking with George Basterfield from Wasdale to Buttermere, that he realised that he might have been right all along. Snow was on the fells and at Scarth Gap, they turned, as so many do, to resurvey the scene before descending into the valley. His crags could clearly be seen and in their centre a pillar stood out against the snow. So it had not been a dream. Although not to have the same explosive consequence, it must have been a similar moment to when Haskett Smith first saw his slender spire of rock momentarily highlighted against a bank of mist, prompting a search for that particular needle in a haystack which would kick-start the beginnings of a sport which spread around the world.

Brown pointed it out to Basterfield who, although certain that if there was anything there it would have been examined long before, promised to give him a day at Easter. On their return, winter was still on the ground and when they reached the foot of the rocks, Brown was both delighted and relieved to see 'the central pillar magnificently rising out of the snow'.[1] Up to that point Basterfield had felt the best they could hope for was a succession of broken rocks that might artificially produce some kind of a route. But it was now clear they had found, if not a major cliff, at least an important minor one situated on the same topographical line as Gable Crag and Pillar Rock. For nomenclature, they consulted local experts and were told the only feature nearby was a knoll called Boat Howe and, as fancy suggested the central pillar resembled a vessel docked in the harbour of the flanking crags, Boat Howe Crags it became, and all the climbs were labelled with appropriate nautical terms.

But that was more than half a century before any ambitions of my own had been born and little likely to be within my grasp had been reported since. Nor was I being unduly pessimistic. Although published many years later, Ken Wilson's *Classic Rock* confirms that scarcely a route, let alone a crag, at that standard and quality had been found since the Second World War. Then, in 1967, news filtered through of a new climb in the Highlands, reputed to be the finest Diff in Britain, with over 500 feet of sustained climbing. It was situated on the south face of the otherwise undistinguished Binnein Shaus, whose only previous claim to fame was featuring in the decision of Queen Victoria to reject Ardverikie House in favour of Balmoral as her country retreat. It is true that crags are marked by the OS but such markings are a common feature of all Highland maps, the majority of which turn out to be no more than a large clump of vegetated boulders. A few excursions soon dampen any enthusiasm for such pointless rampaging through the heather enveloped in a cloud of midges.

As it turned out, Ardverikie Wall was more Severe than Diff but still well within the range of the likes of J H B Bell or W H Murray, neither of whom would have turned down such a challenge. Its location, however, was not that clear. Facing south, it was hidden from the road and there was no obvious reason why hill-goers should wander along the banks of the Lochan na h-Eearba as the area has little to offer the marauding Munroist or other tickers of lists. Moreover, although the A86 lies little more than a mile away, making the crag, by Scottish standards, almost a roadside outcrop, the same thoroughfare is also the retreat route between Fort William and the Cairngorms and tends to attract scuttlers seeking better conditions rather than exploratory sightseers.

Although this discovery rekindled hope and the fruitless search was again initiated, previous experience had blunted the edge. There had been crags closer at hand with substantial sections that seemed to be unclimbed, one in particular, that we pawed at and hovered around, but had been more than a match for our vibram boots and the protection of two full-weight slings. So we soon gave up the unequal struggle, feeling it was the sort of thing that was best left for stickier soles and sturdier minds than ours.

Even when we had found something more amenable, our efforts could hardly be described as successful. Memories of struggles on a rocky encumbrance that overhung an oil-stained river were not encouraging. The outcome of our attempts on this apology for a cliff, that appeared to have sprouted accidentally among the clanging furnaces of busy shipyards, was at the bitter end of any Triumph or Disaster scale. This, in the main, was because our chosen cliff was not (as Menlove Edwards remarked of the similarly decaying Clogwyn y Geifr) the sort of rock to support those 'who rise by seizing every opportunity'. My antics, which included dangling at the end of a rope clutching large detached lumps of sandstone, achieved little other than offer some compensatory amusement for the small boys who had followed me in the hopes of witnessing some spectacular suicide attempt.

But it can't be said such failures caused a weakening of the will. Maps were scanned, false trails followed. Why on earth did Helvellyn not have a crag equal to Scafell or at least Great Gable? It has the height and exposure. Why on the rocky coastline of the North East coast, battered as it was by wind and wave, were there no soaring cliffs to match those of Cornwall or Pembroke? No doubt there is some geological explanation that will satisfy the pedant but it would have been of little comfort to the earnest explorer. Then, one day, I discovered a guide to Pillar Rock and my sense of failure was mollified by alternative dreams.

Mollified but not dismissed. Even today, when the flesh is frail, the same curiosity remains. As I traversed around the retaining walls of the *levadas*—aqueducts that have been hacked into the precipices of Madeiran rock by men who climbed more out of necessity than pleasure—I continued to glance around at the surrounding possibilities. Would that jagged crack reach the slab caught in sunlight? Might the skyline of the sleeping volcano produce another Skye Ridge with inaccessible pinnacles of its own? I realise now that quite a lot had got away. Yet, within that thought, the final line of Fitzgerald's *Gatsby* still drifts through the mind: 'So we beat on, boats against the current, borne back ceaselessly into the past.'

Beginnings

When, post-blitz, the family moved house, my brother and I were delighted to discover that, attached to the premises, was an all-weather sports pitch—or, to put it more precisely, a backyard encased by ten-foot walls. At its western end, this stretch of concrete screeched to a halt at a precipitous drop, the edge of a rather damp void that had been designed to allow light to filter through the cellar window. My father, suspecting at least one of his offspring, probably the smaller, might come to a similarly precipitous end, employed a local bricklayer to build a substantial barrier between the edge of the yard and the abyss. This increase in height meant that if you balanced along the apex of the triangular coping stones, the drop was now a satisfactory twelve feet or so.

The presence of this obstruction caused little concern during the winter months but once the seasons changed and Roker Park was transformed into the headquarters of Marylebone Cricket Club the wall became central to the arcane regulations by which our game of backyard cricket was governed. Architectural foible demanded that the stumps which, to the untutored eye, might have resembled an orange box, had to be placed next to the newly erected rampart and as the descent, aided by a rather rickety stepladder, to the depths of The Pit (for so it was known) was both awkward and unpleasant, losing the ball in its bowels became something of a nuisance. But Invention is born of Necessity. If the batsman through his incompetence edged a delivery over the wall he was not only deemed caught behind but also had the thankless task of retrieving the ball. If, on the other hand, the bowler sufficiently strayed from line and length that the batsman could hook the ball with sufficient skill to ricochet off the boundary wall into the Pit, he was not only awarded four runs but also had the satisfaction of watching his sibling's simian struggles.

Time passed, limbs grew longer and the rickety steps more wretched. As a result, new strategies were deemed necessary to retrieve the succession of tennis balls that found their way into the depths. The steps had balanced on a small platform at mid-point in the descent and with the aid of this and a knee-jarring jump and, on return, a couple of mantleshelf moves, the descent and ascent were easily achieved. There was also a waste pipe on the south face which, coupled with a slightly tricky hand-traverse under the pantry window, provided an alternative point of entry and return. The real challenge, however, was the central wall, apparently holdless and covered in moss.

Closer inspection revealed two possible weaknesses. The bottom eighteen inches, no doubt as a result of mining subsidence, relented from the vertical and at midway point a somewhat tired brick had splintered in two. By edging a foot against the crumbling mortar and placing pressure on downspread palms, it was initially possible to gain a foot or so in height. This allowed a rather tentative reach for the narrow fissure halfway up the wall, where two fingers could be jammed. A semi lay-off encouraged one foot to be pressed against the wall at knee height and, provided these manoeuvres were performed in one continuous movement, sufficient impetus could be generated to stretch for the 'Thank God' hold formed by the coping stone. Thus, in the year when Bradman graced the cricket fields of England for the final occasion, paternal anxiety may well have unwittingly created the original privately owned climbing wall, the genesis of such commercial concerns that now pepper the community.

All the above is a rather roundabout way of introducing a question I have often asked myself. What started my own interest in climbing or, more particularly, in climbing mountains and selected bits of them? Would the pinpointing of *when?* be helped by digging up answers to other questions such as *why?* and *how?* Or was it, as the Italian climber Giusto Gervasutti said in his autobiography, 'rather like trying to remember when one first learnt to swim—somehow one always seems to have known.'[1] Given his own experience, he may well have been right. But it didn't accord with mine. My learning to swim followed formal instruction involving armbands and diving for rubber bricks, and as for mountains my earliest landscape memories were the unevocative flatlands of the Wirral peninsula and the coastal strip that housed the Durham coalfields.

Under these circumstances, the height of summit-bagging was reaching the windmill that bestrode Bidston Hill and the nearest thing to a traverse across an Alpine range was scrabbling around the slag heaps of Monkwearmouth Colliery, so it was not until there was a family holiday in the Lake District that mountains and their attendant possibilities entered my conscious mind. When the young Gervasutti eventually reached the top of his holiday hills, he saw before him 'a whole new unsuspected world: majestic mountains with great sheer walls, or slender spires on which, so it looked from a distance, only an eagle could set foot'.[1] My own view from the top of Helvellyn may not have been as clear-cut as the precipices of the Cadore Dolomites, nor did I see many eagles poised on the slender pinnacles of Striding Edge, but what I did see triggered a reaction that was sufficiently powerful to demand a response over the next six decades.

Rather than delve too deeply into my pre-natal experiences, it might be easier to recall the occasion when, as opposed to wandering uphill, I started rock climbing. There must have been a moment when shinning up trees and Public Monuments metamorphosed into an activity that coincided with the recognised definition of the term. Taking the most direct route to rescue a cragfast little brother springs to mind, as does the ascent of a very big boulder that was lounging around a valley floor in the Lakes. Yet, amongst this confusion, the moment when I *decided* to become a 'rock climber' is not open to question. It was on a hill-walking holiday in the Stubai Alps. Armed with a specific demand from Her Britannic Majesty that all doors should be opened to the bearer, and holding suitable reservations, courtesy of Tyrolean Travel, to go and stay as we pleased, we felt these foreign hills held no terror. After all, had not the mightiest summits of England, Wales and Scotland cowered before our British Commando soles?

At the start all went according to plan. The obvious peaks were conquered, the splodges of paint followed in the approved manner. It was true that the amounts of ascent and descent were greater than in Britain and that smoking a cigarette at 10,000 feet was a less pleasant experience, but otherwise everything seemed straightforward enough. Having climbed the highest peaks, we turned our attention to those of lesser magnitude. At first all was well. There were paths and the occasional daub, but when we parted company from the track that led to the popular Adolphe Pikkler Hutte matters altered. The paths disappeared, the angle steepened, hands came out of pockets. Eventually we reached a blank wall that barred any direct progress. The only way forward was by a rising traverse that appeared to get more and more holdless and more and more poised above a very long drop. No sign of the friendly Herdwick here, whose bulk might break your fall. I pawed at the rock, Phil pawed at the rock. But it was of no use. We were stymied and, as this was clearly a door too far even for Her Britannic Majesty, yesterday's heroes of the hour, whose ascent of the 'mighty' Harbicht had so impressed the packaged middle-aged tourists in the *Gasthof*, had no alternative but to return to the valley and reassemble their egos with the aid of rotwein and schnapps. We were also in no doubt that if we were to go higher and further, we would have to learn the ropes.

The confusion of our early climbing experience (the gibes of sharp-tongued infants; swimming up unfathomable routes on Lower Kern Knotts) before finally reaching the summit of Pillar Rock has been all too well documented. It wasn't a very impressive Grand Tour, but at least we had done it ourselves. Today's beginner, swaddled in helmet and harness, is marched up routes which sixty years ago would have been the ultimate ambition of most climbers. Sticky shoes and the appropriate dose of bling and bong can quickly cut most pre-war classics down to size. Reconsidering these alternatives, I realise that, through force of circumstance, I fell completely in line with Gervasutti's second opinion that by not joining a club he 'had found the finer experience [of coming] to mountaineering gradually, with no fixed ideas and definite intentions, my only motive to please myself.'[1]

These were the matches that lit the fire, but what was the kindling that sustained it? Mountaineers tended not to flock to my coastal plain, so I had no model to follow or local hero to inspire. Instead, books would have to be my mentor. They came not from bookshops, which seemed to offer little other than John Hunt's epic account, but from the local library which was surprisingly well stocked, or from among the occasional mouldering heaps of a house clearance. Murray's *Mountaineering in Scotland* and *Undiscovered Scotland* set the pulse racing. Oppenheimer's *The Heart of Lakeland* rekindled old memories, *Rock Climbing in Skye* by Ashley Abraham promised riches beyond any dream that the military manoeuvres of the future Baron Hunt of Llanfair Waterdine could possibly suggest. For ambience, I relied on Harry Griffin's accounts of the Lake District, the nearest and dearest of my climbing grounds. For history and tradition there was Clark and Pyatt's *Mountaineering in Britain*, then later, Byne and Sutton's *High Peak*. But, above all these, was Gervasutti's autobiography. When it came to books on climbing, his was first in the queue.

Paradoxically, the books of formal instruction which should be most useful to the beginner probably teach you least about mountains and mountaineering. You cannot question their worthiness. There are diagrams of every knot under the sun, illustrations of how to arrest a fall in winter and pictures of the inner workings of map and compasses. Leaders demonstrate each grip and jam known to man and Second Men stand solemnly at their belays, paying out rope in the then approved manner. Like telephone directories and recipe books, they are very useful in their way, yet scarcely bedtime reading.

There are exceptions. Gaston Rébuffat's *On Snow and Rock* inspired, mainly through the photographs used to illustrate his instructional text. You have little soul if you are not fired by the geometric combination of rock and space, glistening ice against a cloudless sky, with the climber, exuding Gallic nonchalance, poised on the edge of all things. For local colour, there was Colin Kirkus' *Let's Go Climbing*, part of a series designed to enthuse the young with a desire for healthy pastimes. Kirkus, like some older cousin, gathers his readers in the crook of his arm, issuing warnings by citing his own follies and hinting at hidden treats that will be their reward after they have mastered the cheerfully explained basics.

In fact, it was probably the climbing guidebooks rather than the teach-yourself manuals that were of the most practical use to the uninitiated. They not only told you where routes were but also what you could expect to find when you got there. Of course, the descriptions presented their own problems. How difficult was a 'Difficult'? What particular malicious nature was implied by a 'fierce-looking' crack, an 'awkward' step or a slope at an 'unpleasant' angle? But for us they had a saving grace. It was the practice in early guides, particularly those produced by the Fell and Rock, for the climbs to be listed in ascending order of severity, so there was no danger of our assuming that, because they were within the same grade, the ability to climb a Severe route teetering on the edge of V Diff meant that another knocking at the VS door was automatically within our capabilities. In addition, guidebooks often had a hidden agenda to give a sense of place and atmosphere, not only in their introductions, but in the route descriptions themselves. These veered from the helpful, 'a useful introduction to the grade', through the provocative, 'the route meanders to avoid the main difficuties', to the downright sarcastic, 'experience in grass and bad rock, if not gained before, is likely to be early fostered on Clogwyn y Geifr'.

But even there I was not dealt the best of hands. When I first started climbing, guidebooks were thin on the ground. Most were out of date and seemed to be out of print or very hard to find. I did my first serious rock climbing on Pillar Rock because it was the only guide I could lay my hands on. The guide to the local Northumbrian Crags was nowhere to be seen and even today I have never seen for sale a second-hand copy of that particular edition. North

Wales was even worse. The existing guide covering the Llanberis Pass and Clogwyn Du'r Arddu had been printed before the War and, although there was sufficient development to merit Peter Harding's interim 'Bumper Fun Book', the whole area was not entirely brought up to date until 1966.

But all was not lost. I cast my library net more widely and where this meant visits to places where I had no 'Rights to Borrow', I copied wholesale into a series of notebooks. There are not many crags where I have climbed every route but, as a result of my researches, those listed by Eric Byne in his *Climbing Guide to Brassington Rocks* is one of them. Then, on our first visit to North Wales, we struck gold. By chance we stayed at a B&B run by Scotty Dwyer, a professional climbing guide and, of course, he had every guidebook available, augmented by type-written sheets describing recent developments. When he realised that we were there to climb and not just two lads on a spree, he was most forthcoming with the necessary information. With his guides to hand, it was easy enough to plan our campaign on a day-by-day basis. It didn't always work out perfectly. At the start, fuelled by the self-belief which only an evening in the Bryn Tyrch can give, routes were chosen, only to discover in the cold light of day that much of our choice, so assiduously copied in longhand, was beyond our abilities. Fortunately, some of the easier routes were obvious to deduce and our ambition was reduced to more sober proportions.

Even if this gives some idea about my own beginnings, clearly I was not the first to discover the delights of ascending steep rock. There is a greater and more interesting question: why should anyone, given the obvious dangers, begin to climb at all? Answers vary. Gervasutti's explanation is that he was 'above all determined to overcome the fear and uneasiness of the valley-dweller'.[1] Mallory offered a somewhat more prosaic response. There is no doubt that, for some people, uneasy with the implications of formal religions and social conformity, mountains provide a mystical experience and an existential or alternative lifestyle. For others, the pleasure of companionship is made all the more poignant by the real possibility of a sudden and violent parting. For most, I suspect, it is a rattle-bag of reasons, where due proportion is decided according to the mood of the moment

There is also no doubt that some people are motivated by dreams of personal glory. 'The first man to' has a seductive ring and, with its clearly defined targets, climbing is an attractive proposition for the egotist in us all. In most activities, we quickly realise exactly what sort of stuff dreams are made of and turn to alternative pastimes, but it is at this point that climbing plays its trump card and reveals its hidden charm to turn what might have been a short, albeit fierce, flirtation into a lifelong passion.

Regardless of grade, the individual challenge is the same. When I all too quickly reached my limitations and realised the unlikelihood of future guidebooks being liberally sprinkled with my achievements, a comforting thought struck me. As with me, there must be a point where even Joe Brown found something difficult/desperate/impossible, just as I had. Of course, it would not be same point but the satisfaction he felt when he overcame/controlled/circumnavigated the problem could be no more or less than mine in similar circumstances. In real terms, the off-balance single-finger press-up of the master cragsman is no harder or easier than is the layback to the beginner. Equally comforting, when you are struggling to get off the ground, is the knowledge that even the best are not always perfect. After a bad day I can take considerable comfort from a re-reading of Menlove Edwards' essay, 'A Great Effort' (CCJ 1941).

It could be argued that it is the same for most sports and that scoring a goal or striking the ball to the boundary against inferior opposition is the same for the less competent as it is for an international in a Test match or FA Cup Final. Golf, in particular, tries through a subtle piece of self-deception (aka the handicap system) to pretend that the weak are as skilful as the strong, but it requires a certain type of mental agility to persuade yourself that a Parks pitch is the same as Wembley or Lords, or that you have won the race when you have been given a head start. In climbing, rabbit and tiger alike share the same view, feel the same atmosphere, suffer the same sense of exposure and are prey to the same weather and the foibles of their nature. They take and accept the same risks. These similarities are heightened when climbing solo, the original and most pure form of the sport, where, if something irredeemable happens you are, as C E Montague has it, likely to be subject to 'nasty "obiter dicta" during the inquest'. The philosophical Giusto sums it up nicely, when after a lone struggle on a brutish pitch in the Dolomites, he eventually hauls himself to safety: 'It was I, and I alone, who had sought this moment of suspense, created it, compelled it.'[1]

So, on the matter of 'beginnings', this leaves us with a final question. When did we start to climb? Man has always tried to command the high ground for military, religious and economic purposes. The Romans marched their legions along the High Street range of the Lake District, saints set up retreats on rock-strewn mountain slopes and shepherds no doubt struggled with the technical intricacies of gullies and slabs to rescue over-ambitious sheep. Yet, just as there must have been a moment when mankind looked at the five fish it had caught and the five fingers that had caught them and discovered the concept and beauty of number, so there must have been a moment when climbing turned from a chore to a pleasure.

Most sports have their roots in youthful games devised to encourage the skills necessary to overcome the difficulties of adult life. These can vary from simple rough-and-tumble and variants of hide-and-seek to evolved, complex games like rugby football which developed sophisticated rules to produce the mental agility and strength of character to run an extensive Empire. It was assumed that if you could stay calm under a high ball in Twickenham, when the might of the Celtic hordes bore down on you with serious intent, running one of Her Majesty's Colonies would be a bagatelle. Sir Henry Newbolt's poem 'Vitaï Lampada' gives the general idea for those who have not had the dubious advantage of such an upbringing.

Lacking this essential *esprit de corps*, climbing seems an unlikely candidate to become an organised sport. But there is more than sufficient evidence to suggest acts of daring were a formal rite of youthful passage, and climbing difficult pieces of rock was one of them. An ascent of the Eagle Stone behind Baslow Edge, for example, was apparently seen as evidence of fitness for marriage. Though when reaching its summit moved from an adolescent imperative to an adult sport is rather harder to gauge. All we can say is that in 1900 the Kyndwr Club, encouraged by J W Puttrell, made a successful combined assault on the rock without, as far as can be ascertained, the inducement of love-lorn maidens to spur them on.

In any event, for a youthful rite to pass into the ritual of an adult sport is essentially a matter of socio-economics. If the tribe was of the hunter/gatherer variety, all the available daylight was spent searching for food and any shinning up rocks was only to escape rampaging mastodons. But when suitable conditions allowed an agrarian society to flourish, the food supply was controlled. As a result, a proportion of the tribe had time to develop more sophisticated skills and interests. Thus empowered, they were able to exert their influence which meant, as often as not, planting their flags on other people's property. The Brits were particularly keen on this but when it came to planting them on the top of mountains, they decided, being British, to make it a game.

As George Orwell pointed out in his essay 'The Sporting Spirit', games can easily take on a more sinister aspect. National prestige as well as individual achievement was at stake. Not surprisingly, some of the locals objected to hobnailed boots trampling over what they regarded as sacred ground and, as mountain ranges form part of natural geographical barriers, the underlying struggle for territorial control was never far from the surface. Such was the confusion of politics, religion and jingoism that it is almost impossible to work out in a historical sense when any mountain was climbed for its own sake.

Yet it might be possible, however, to trace the history of one sub-set of mountaineering, i.e. rock climbing, as a separate sport. The place was the Lake District and the date was July 9th, 1826. Although, as with nearly all British mountains, the Cumbrian summits could easily be reached by an able-bodied tourist, there were two pieces of local rock that demanded a certain amount of climbing skill. The first was Broad Stand, a rock-step that barred a direct route from the highest point in England to its parent mountain, Scafell. The second, and more important, was Pillar Rock, the nearest thing in England to an inaccessible mountain summit. This detached mass was guarded by rock ramparts on all sides, some of which fell for over 400 feet before they reached relatively easy ground. The challenge was obvious and on the day in question John Atkinson made the first ascent via the west face. Once the top had been gained, the rules of the game were modified to finding alternative and, ideally, more challenging ways of reaching the summit and in 1863 a successful attack on the east was recorded.

The idea of searching out and climbing different bits of rock regardless of height seemingly caught on. As early as 1885, an article appeared in *All the Year Round*, a magazine edited by Charles Dickens Jnr, entitled 'The Climbs of the English Lake District' in which the author, C N Williamson, described, with particular reference to Pillar, the history of the sport and other various rock-climbing possibilities of the district. The article was reprinted in the first Journal of the Fell and Rock Climbing Club with the comment that 'its perusal was the incentive to many who afterwards became keen and well-known cragsmen'.[2]

One such was Walter Parry Haskett Smith who, in 1881, was a member of a university reading party at Wasdale Head. There would have been times when the view through the window meant the products of Parnassus were abandoned for the more immediate attraction of the local hills and, led by the energetic F

H Bowring, the party roamed the district, examining the cliffs and gullies. Haskett Smith must have been impressed for, the following year, he returned and completed several new ascents on a variety of crags. The interesting thing is that, unlike his contemporaries, he did these climbs not as preparation for the Alps, which he had never visited, but for their own sake. Most led to no summit but finished when the climbing difficulties ran out. By the end of the century, his experience allowed him to produce *Climbing in the British Isles* which listed each and every known climbing possibility in the country.

Inspired by his efforts, others joined the race and by the turn of the century eighty separate climbs in the Lake District had been recorded. Simultaneously, the Abraham brothers, through their dramatic photographs, spread the Gospel and, with O G Jones, produced a comprehensive survey of the climbs in the Lake District, North Wales and Skye. After that, it was only a matter of time before Clubs sprang into existence to form the backbone of an activity that is followed to this day. And, as these stuttering beginnings seem curiously to resemble my own, it appears a good point to bring this investigation to a close.

Naming and Shaming

It wasn't long after I started to climb that I realised there was a bit more to it than putting one hand in front of another. There was clearly an etiquette, an unwritten code of how to behave. Just as the synonyms 'mount', 'struggle up', 'conquer', 'clamber', 'soar' and 'skylark' are to be found in a thesaurus, each suggesting a variety of approaches to climbing lumps of grass, rock and ice, so there is a multiplicity of reasons for any one individual's interest in the pastime. It is, therefore, of little surprise that there are conflicting views on how the climber should behave.

Let's take two pronouncements I have come across at one time or another: *(a)* the sort of man who would drive a piton into English rock is the sort of man who would shoot a fox, and *(b)* people who rest on slings are useless 'doggers' who should stick to routes within their ability. Both reveal types with particularly strident views. The first was a commonly held attitude by those who believed that sport in general was the prerogative of the leisured classes, a belief augmented by the assumption that any attempt by Johnny Foreigner to prove himself better must in some way involve cheating. The second typifies the 'laddish'

30

banter employed by competitive young males and is aimed at belittling the better efforts of others.

What is interesting in the existence of these comments is not so much that they illustrate a divergence of types, but that a reactionary member of the landed gentry and a crag rat should have so much in common. Both assumed, apparently without question, that each had the prerogative to decide how others should behave. They had in some way claimed the right to pontificate on the 'proper' way to climb as if they owned the moral high ground that belonged to the debate. In essence, what both are saying is: 'If you can't do it my way, you've no right to do it yours.'

What neither seemed to have thought through was the logical outcome of the argument. As the law stands, the only person who has a *right* to 'drive a piton into English rock' is the owner of the rock in question. If the less expert 'dogger' had already purchased the cliff, he might have advised his tormentor to stick his views in an appropriate place. With this in mind, I suggest that such comments are provoked less by a sense of moral indignation than the attitude the dog displayed towards the manger. More succinctly, that any general judgement on the rights and wrongs in climbing method should be tempered by an awareness that special interests could be at play.

The giving of names, for example, often has an ulterior motive. The slave-owner did not bestow his surname on his human possessions as an act of familial inclusion and it can be assumed that star-struck parents hope their name-borrowing might sprinkle some of the original's charisma over their offspring. As this sort of motive is not unconnected with a desire to own, it is worth considering whether the names awarded to individual climbs carry with them a similar hidden agenda.

In the first instance, naming was simply topographical. 'Left Hand Gully' distinguished the climb from a similar configuration at the right-hand end of the cliff. Climbs were given proper names but these were born as a shorthand version of the chimney that Smith climbed, rather than Smith claiming the fissure as his own. But matters soon changed. Once the obvious had been eliminated and the stock of alphabet slabs and benumbered buttresses had been exhausted, a more playful mood prevailed. Given that climbing was, for the most part, the preserve of the educated classes, humour in the forms of puns and scholarly erudition began to emerge. Kipling's Groove was so named because it was 'ruddy 'ard' and the followers of Nebs's Crawl on Dinas y Gromlech were prewarned that, like the King of Babylon, they may be forced to negotiate an awkward passage through the long grass. Perhaps Godiva Groove, 'somewhat exposed in the upper section', more or less sums up the tone.

Eventually, the generally shared witticisms petered out and the origin of names became the private jokes of the protagonists. As J H Doughty wondered in his essay on 'Nomenclature', 'what curses first rent Blasphemy Crack, what orgies initiated the Cocktail Route?'[1] The culmination of the enigmatic was probably reached with a climb on the Roaches entitled Reset Portion of Galley 37, though whether the compositor was complicit in this unique contribution to the history of climbing in Britain is not on record. There seems little doubt, however, that the choice of names helped maintain the aura of an exclusive group who saw the hills and the climbs upon them as their particular preserve.

Unsurprisingly, this playing with words and meaning began to develop a more political subplot. The naming of Borstal Buttress, that complements the nearby Oxford and Cambridge Climb, could scarcely have been accidental and when Brown and Whillans snatched a plum route on Carn Dearg, to howls of Celtic abuse emanating from the CIC hut, their decision to christen it Sassenach must have carried with it a certain resonance. And, in line with this spirit of general bolshiness, it was almost inevitable that, with the emergence of substantial numbers of working-class climbers, there would be a backlash against the likes of Doctor's Dilemma and Pedagogues' Chimney.

Equally inevitably, this desire to scratch the proletariat mark on the rock face of climbing history led to a collision with the proprietorial assumptions of the established clubs in the area. The tradition had been established, probably through a mixture of deference and a desire for notoriety, of registering a new route with the local senior club which, in turn, would include it in their appropriate guidebook. It soon became clear, however, that the potentate and the parvenu had rather different ideas when it came to suitability of nomenclature. As Bill Smith, a member of the Creagh Dhu, complained: whenever they sent details of their new climbs to the SMC, 'this bloke called Bell wouldn't have it, he was always objecting to the names of the routes or something like that'.[2]

What is a surprise, is that a similar situation might have arisen some forty years before. In 1919 H M Kelly and C F Holland completed two parallel routes on the west face of Pillar Rock. The ascent of the second was not without its problems. While manipulating the rope over a projection, Kelly managed to knock

Holland's 'most precious climbing companion'[3] from his mouth and send it spinning into the void below. To add injury to insult, he then disturbed some loose rock which drew blood and some rather acerbic comments from his second. In Holland's obituary, Kelly remarked on a certain coolness and how he had been relieved when, on the return journey, Holland suggested that, as they 'were not to be looked back upon',[3] the two new routes should be christened Sodom and Gomorrah. It is clear that for some reason this was regarded as unacceptable for they materialised in the handwritten account of the Wasdale Climbing Book under the more prosaic titles of Route I and Route II and appeared as such in the guidebook. If this change of heart was the result of possible official disapproval, it is a pity. The choice of names was probably as much a typically understated apology by Holland for his recent ill-temper as it was a reference to the heinous sins condemned by the Old Testament.

From the start, guidebooks writers labelled each route with a headline consisting of its name and other basic information. You quickly learn to distinguish between the various parts, as misconstruing the nature of a route carrying the appellation, 'A Piece of Cake', might easily lead the novice to bite off a bit more than he could chew. To discover the actual difficulty of any particular climb, it is necessary to examine the grade of difficulty awarded to it. You would imagine that such a system by its very nature could not be perfidious. If a rock climb is classified as Easy, it must be and, save for the physically handicapped, would be regarded as such by the majority of hill-goers. But the mystery deepens as you move up the grades. In the beginning, when chaos made way for light, there were three grades: Easy, Difficult and Severe. To distinguish the various shades of hindrance, modifiers such as Moderately, Just, Hard and Very were added. But such contortions of expression did this conjure up, that before long apparent contradictions such as Easy Severe and Mild Very Difficult began to appear. Even in normal conversation between climbers, the phrase 'quite difficult' could mean anything from 'not much to it' to 'more to it than meets the eye', according to the accompanying tone of voice or facial expression. On the page there are no such aids, so it was not long before the voice of reason was added to the tongues of babble.

Its proponents wanted to produce a more logical approach, pointing out that the range of adjectives would eventually slide off the hyperbolic scale. Robin Smith, in typically caustic manner, makes the point. He explains that, below the Border, the English had climbs they call XS, where 'X is a variable from exceptionally or extremely, through very or hardly, to merely or mildly severe'.[4] That Smith's wit emanated from Scotland is not entirely surprising for, as a climbing race, the Scots had a particular sense of gallows humour. For many years they refused to grade any route, regardless of relative difficulty, above Very Severe. This was not very helpful for English visitors who were assured that just above cloud level was a 'a nice wee VS', only to find it was as technically difficult as any Extreme in the Pass and probably in a rather more primeval state. All very confusing and, one suspects, intended to be so. If pressed to explain, the SMC tended to withdraw into the mists of discussion that surround the mutabilty of Scottish weather.

Eventually horns were grabbed and in 1942 the Great Grading Debate was launched. J E Q Barford and J M Edwards produced an article in the Climbers' Club Journal which explained the workings of and reasons for the new system of gradation which had appeared in the most recent guide to Clogwyn Du'r Arddu. In simple terms, the current adjectival system was to be replaced by a numerical system that arranged the existing climbs into six divisions, each with two alphabetical subdivisions. The obvious advantages were the lack of verbal clutter and the ease with which the six classes could be extended if significantly harder climbs were completed. It was also pointed out that a fresh start created an ideal opportunity for the Fell and Rock and SMC to follow suit, so producing a much needed uniform system throughout Britain.

The response was immediate. In the Journal of the following year, a selection of members aired their views. As was to be expected from a Club which had been suspicious of guidebooks from the outset, the response was for the most part conservative and was summed up by G F Peaker who suggested, quoting their wartime Prime Minister, that members should 'beware of needless innovations, particularly when inspired by logic'.[5] The objections centred not around the relative merits of alternate systems but *(a)* the lack of respect for the pioneers, *(b)* that it was little more than rebranding an existing system and *(c)* the danger of an open-ended scale which would lead to 'breakneck rivalries'.[5]

Under the cover of moral indignation can be discerned, as with names, a more subtle reason, this time launched by conservative nostalgia. R M Hamer, separated from his homeland, lamenting the loss of adjectives for 'horrid figures', declared, 'I will still like to think of some day achieving again a mild severe—not a IVB'[5] and R A Mallet produced a cleverly wrought poem entitled 'Tell Me Not In Mournful Numbers', urging the bulk of the membership to rebel against anyone 'who, without a semblance of apology / Has wished on us this blasted numeralogy'.[6] These and similar comments show that many climbers at the time put considerable store by some extraneous quality associated with the existing grading system. The choice of adjective was not simply a matter of classification, but served an additional need. It had not taken long for the adjectives to change into proper nouns which had their own coded meaning. A severe climb became more specifically a Severe. The grades below had the affectionate contraction (Diff and V Diff) that comes with easy acquaintance. The top grade was simple VS, an unexplained yet adulatory use of initials reminiscent of the likes of A1 or VIP. In 1943, the phrase 'he's a VS man' had its own cachet and was spoken in the reverential terms more usually reserved for statesmen and captains of industry.

As it happened, if change were needed there already existed in the climbing world a perfectly good system to cover most of the objections. Each climb was given an overall adjectival description that reflected the general difficulty, taking into account length, state of the rock, protectability and such like, along with a numerical grade that assessed the technical or gymnastic skill needed to overcome the more holdless sections. It had been rejected by the climbing establishment who, still basking in the dying sun of imperial glory, clung to the myth that, as Britain was the originator of all sports and pastimes, it should be the sole arbiter of their rules and protocol. Besides, the system was practised by such races as the Germans and Italians, whose sense of climbing propriety was thought to be, at best, misguided. As well as citing, albeit ill-advisedly, the Continental preference to support his suggestion, Barford pointed out that the numerical system was also used in the SMC guide to Skye. The Scots, no doubt alarmed at the thought they might be falling in line with the English, immediately reverted to the adjectival method.

Eventually an uneasy truce emerged. As we have seen, the adverbs 'Extremely' and 'Exceptionally' had been introduced to indicate climbs substantially more difficult than 'Very' Severe, and this was seamlessly abbreviated to the letter E. As harder and harder climbs were successfully attempted, each step-up in standard was given an ever-increasing number. Thus, serious climbers were given infinitely expanding targets from a baseline of E1, while their lesser brethren could be left to browse contentedly amongst the Moderately Perilous and the Frankly Disappointings.

The third and final piece of headline information —the length of the climb—seems at first sight a simple statement of fact and unlikely to cause any controversy. In reality, this figure represented the length of the individual pitches when added together, yet these individual lengths carried a message of their own. It is rare for a climb, or even a section of a climb, to be uniformly difficult and, when roped climbing started, it made a great deal of difference as to how far the leader would fall before this descent was arrested. The chances of survival following a slip on a twenty-foot pitch were considerably greater than a similar mishap near the top of one eighty feet longer. Once the climber emerged from the gully epoch, the opportunities of finding a staircase of commodious ledges with convenient pinnacles around which to belay became less and less likely and climbs inevitably became more and more dangerous.

The simple solution was to shorten the pitches artificially, so reducing the run-out between pitches to manageable proportions. At first, this consisted of hitching the 'live' rope behind a flake of rock or threading it around chockstones that had jammed in fissures of various widths. If such protection occurred close to the crux of the climb, then it effectively reduced the climb to something akin to a boulder problem and, inevitably, questions surfaced as to the sporting morality of such practices. The real difficulty arose when the device was used for a more underhand purpose. With a little tension, the climber could rest and inspect the problem at his leisure. Worse still, a rope sling placed above an unscrupulous climber could be put to a variety of uses.

Matters came to a head when, in 1936, members of a party from Bavaria hammered their barbarous spikes into the wall of Tryfan's East Face. The completion of Munich Climb produced cries of protest at the desecration of British rock through the insertion of foreign bodies and, as importantly, at the avoidance of natural difficulty by employing artificial aid to assist their ascent. Probably the most sectarian chapter of this attitude was the reaction to the appearance of the karabiner, which was regarded as even more dastardly than the piton. The objection was twinfold. First, it was a mechanical device, a machine that destroyed the bond between Man and Nature and, second and more tellingly, the word had no etymological connection with any in the English language. Matters could only have got worse if Hitler had decided to drive up Snowdon on a motorbike.

Among the clamour nothing seems to have been mentioned of Jack Longland previously completing the crux of his eponymous climb on Cloggy with the aid of an inserted chockstone that had, with malice aforethought, been transported to the spot in Morley Wood's rucksack. Or that the early ascents of the Central Buttress of Scafell had only been secured when various parts of the seconds' anatomy were used, at first passively to gain height and then actively as a vice to secure a foothold where none existed, thus managing a multiplicty of *Vorsprung durch Technik* which even the most ingeniously designed German piton had yet managed to master. And when it came to desecrating British rock, eyes were closed to the exploits of a member of no less than the Alpine Club who had, a generation before, hacked a chunk out of the same cliff to provide the crucial foothold on the first ascent of Moss Ghyll.

Far from maintaining a state of moral grace, it seemed British resourcefulness knew no bounds when it came to gaining an advantage in the race for first ascents. Perhaps the most bizarre attempt was the time L G Shadbolt tried to train limpets to provide a sturdy alternative to the conventional method of progress. He reported in the Climbers' Club Journal of 1912 that he had discovered on the native cliffs of the island of Sark, that the 'more robust specimens may be used as footholds if due warning is given of the coming strain ... but, in spite of careful nourishment, they refused to stick to unknown rock faces at the word of command'.[7] For the purist who still hankers after the Golden Age, it must be some comfort to know that, at a time when long-cherished values were seeping away, the British Limpet still aspired to the Corinthian spirit of fair play.

Eventually, the adoption of double standards was buttressed by that other great British trait, compromise. Initially, it was accepted that pitons could be used on first ascents 'for protection only', then, provided the sin was admitted, for actual aid to complete the climb. In this way, an historical sub-set came into being, with guidebooks not only crediting the first ascent (FA) which allowed the use of the original number of pitons but also the first ascent freed from aid (FFA), after which point it was no longer acceptable to use artificial aid to complete the climb. Eventually these distinctions reached Byzantine proportions. Questions arose. Can you say you have properly led a route if you *(a)* first inspected it on a top rope, *(b)* pre-placed protection, *(c)* yo-yoed up and down the hard bits until you discovered the right sequence of moves? As we have seen, these matters generated a fair amount of disparagement, inspired less by reasoned argument, more a consequence of territorial jealousy. Even the fundamental logic seems suspect. It was deemed perfectly reasonable for an expert to use protection or aid when he found himself 'in extremis'. But it was supposed that lesser mortals when reaching their point of no return should do the proper thing and (like the limpets) fall to oblivion. If one man could with impunity place a piton to climb Cenotaph Corner, why should another not place one on the Ordinary Route of Idwal Slabs?

Curiously, there was a type of rock that seemed to escape these strictures. At one time it was deemed perfectly reasonable for even the rank incompetent to hammer pitons, wedges, or any other gear Ellis Brigham might have had on its shelves into the limestone outcrops that flourish in the White Peak. Why this distinction occurred is difficult to say. A R Thomson's description of Herford's first free ascent of Ilam Rock (the real first ascent was done with the aid of a rope thrown over the summit) might offer something in the way of explanation. When his second followed, part of the cliff weighing 'certainly several hundred-weights'[8] collapsed beneath him, leaving him hanging from tufts of grass that fortunately held his weight. Although the climb was completed, the rock was judged 'desperately rotten'[8] and the author considered the climb the 'most arduous and insecure' that he had done. No doubt readers of the Rucksack Journal thought if the conqueror of the most difficult climbs in the Lake District had considered the undertaking somewhat dodgy, limestone was to be avoided wherever possible and that if you were brave/foolish enough to try it, you were equally entitled to take such measures as were necessary to safeguard, if not your moral welfare, at least your life and limb.

The use of aid was steadily reduced and many of the artificial climbs were gradually freed up. The three artificial routes on Ilam Rock recorded in the first limestone guidebook to the Peak were graded at A1 or A2. They are now considered to be E2 and E3 and are entirely free from any necessity for ironmongery. Perhaps this *laissez-faire* attitude began to shake a belief which had, in any event, started to crumble more quickly than the rock that surrounded it. As climbing, at least in Britain, moved across the spectrum from the exploration of unknown cliffs, often in vile weather, to rock gymnastics when conditions allowed, the use of aid was at last seen in a different light. As the old century ended, the advent of 'sport climbing' allowed pre-bolted routes to be enjoyed in sunnier climes and comparative safety. At home, aid was used as a legitimate method to increase standards; abroad it became a necessary adjunct to the serious climber's armoury. And so, the Great Debate quietly faded away.

There was a curious postscript to all this. In 1968 the whole business of the ethics surrounding aid was given a different perspective. A 'Mystery Climber' appeared who laid claim to a number of first ascents on the cliffs of Anglesey. The most notable of these was Afreet Street on Gogarth, which seemed to have pushed standards well above the existing limit. Suspicions were aroused as to the veracity of the climber's account. Not least because he did not appear to be up to the part physically and his seconds always disappeared before they could confirm his claims. It would not be the first time it had been thought that 'new routes' had been accomplished with the aid of binoculars. Forces were rallied and later inspection proved the routes described had clearly not been climbed at all. At which point the Mystery Climber vanished into thin air. But he left a point to ponder. In this world of smoke and mirrors, it seems the greatest of all climbing aids is the imagination which can invent names, grades and points of aid at will. A piece of artifice that is not only beyond policing but, to gratify the pure of soul, leaves not a single mark on the hallowed surface of British Rock.

Second to None

It would be generally agreed that any man who sets out to forge his birth certificate is up to no good. But Cecil Frederick (Charles) Holland was not 'any man' and his intention to deceive had an entirely honourable motive. Born in 1886, he had fought with distinction in the First World War and at the outburst of the second set of hostilities immediately volunteered for active service. His alteration of the date on which he entered this world was based on an assumption that he was a better judge of whether a man was fit for active service than some desk-bound arbitrator in the War Office. Nor was this act of defiance the first occasion he had challenged authority.

As he explained in an article for the Climbers' Club Journal entitled 'How I Began to Climb', he would, rather than grace the playing fields of Westminster School in 'a futile game of soccer',[1] abscond to the school library to pore over a recent and exciting discovery. Anyone who has risked the experience of 'cutting organised exercise' in a public boarding school will realise that this was the act of an either very determined or a very foolish young man. What held his attention and chanced the wrath of officialdom was a large black tome with the unequivocal title *Rock-Climbing in the Lake District* by one Owen Glynne Jones, BSc. Lond. which by happy chance he had first opened at an action photograph of Napes Needle suitably decorated with a smattering of snow.

I suspect the whole of Holland's life was punctuated with similar non-conformist moments. H R C Carr, in a tribute to his friend and one-time colleague, tells the story of how, during his early training in the First World War, the new recruits had to face a kit inspection. Inevitably, the Sergeant Major peacocked along the line, determined to put an early stamp on his authority. A close examination of Holland's assembled pieces of equipment led to the question of whether he had any regulation blacking. 'No,' replied Holland. Drawing upon generations of contempt that the regular army had for conscripts, the Sergeant Major filled his lungs and in an ever-rising crescendo bellowed, 'No—WHAT?' 'No—blacking' was the insouciant reply.

This level of self-confidence had not always been with him. His enthusiasm for the doings of O G Jones and his peer group existed at a theoretical rather than practical level, as he was certain he would not have the nerve to follow in their footholds. It wasn't the loneliness of the mountains that put him off. Indeed, he spent his free time cycling around the remotest of places searching for 'the hidden source of content and happiness'[1] without which he felt life was not worth living. Eventually his quest led to Alpine winter sports and, by chance, this provided the moment he sought. His third season produced insufficient snow to ski, or even toboggan, so, on the spur of the moment, he decided to hire a guide and have a crack at a peak with 'a thousand odd feet of steep rocks to be ascended and descended'.[1] The feat duly accomplished, he knew that, after many years of prodding and poking, he had found the pot at the end of his rainbow.

Encouraged by this success, Holland returned to England to buy a pair of nailed boots and a copy of George Abraham's *British Mountain Climbs*. One final cycle tour was undertaken but on this occasion the search for the 'magic casement'[1] was no longer random and one wet and no doubt windy day he arrived at the portals of Ogwen Cottage. He, in his own words, 'stalked in and announced to the assembled company … that I wanted to climb and would somebody please show me how.'[1] It says much for the inmates who, through bitter experience, had decided a day spent in front of the fire was preferable to whatever sea of troubles the Nant Ffrancon could throw at them, that the demand was not turned down flat. For, as Holland continued to report, 'Within an hour Mr F C Aldous was piloting me up the Milestone Buttress.'[1] At last, the harbour half glimpsed among the dusty stacks of a London school library had been reached.

Holland's good fortune did not stop there. On a following trip to the promised land he travelled by train from Bangor to Bethesda. Opposite him sat a tall young man of striking appearance who clearly was not one of the locals. They shared a cab to Ogwen and the ensuing conversation gave Holland an entrée to the élite of Britain's climbing fraternity. As the stranger had arrived a day before the rest of his party, he invited his travelling companion to join him on an expedition to the cliffs of Glyder Fawr. The stranger was Siegfried Herford.

They must have got on well as Holland was invited at Easter of the following year to join Herford and his companions at Wasdale. He could have scarcely believed his luck. Herford, along with with G S Sansom, had designs on the vast central buttress of Scafell that separated Moss Ghyll from Botterill's Slab and during the summer of 1913 had worked out a Girdle Traverse of the whole cliff, in the course of which they climbed out of Moss Ghyll into the very heart of the unclimbed face. The route landed on a commodious ledge which they christened The Oval, presumably to distinguish the size of its 'playing' area from the well-known Tennis Court they had just vacated.

Rising above them was a large flange that an age of frost and ice had prised from the parent rock. This Great Flake was to be the key to any successful attempt on the central buttress and in April 1914 the first efforts were launched. Not only was the climb technically difficult, it also required complicated rope tactics. On 19th April, with H B Gibson and Holland manipulating the ropes above and below, Herford and Samson finally unlocked the problem. They had, however, by this time expended their reserves of energy (Holland had spent seven hours on the Oval) so, leaving a rope in position, they returned the next day when the Great Flake was finally vanquished and the route completed. As a result, on 20th April 1914, CFH who should, by the climbing mores of the time, have been working his way through the Moderately Difficults, became a member of the triumphant party who had been the first to ascend what, at the time, was the hardest climb in Britain.

Not long afterwards, the outbreak of war put paid to any further opportunities to climb. Although Holland had been involved at the cutting edge of Lake District climbing, he was, by his own admission, thoroughly frightened and little more than excess baggage for the party. In his description of his struggles to climb the Flake, which involved a multiplicity of ropes and assorted knots, he chose to 'draw a veil'[2] and there is no reason to believe any other than the assessment of an editor of the Climbers' Club Journal that, at the time, he was no more than a very average climber. But once the war was over everything changed. Within two years he had become the first man to lead a new route on Scafell, so adding his name to an illustrious élite which comprised Haskett Smith, O G Jones and Siegfried Herford, had solved the last great problem in the Ogwen Valley and, with H M Kelly and C G Crawford on Pillar Rock, added seven new climbs, two at the highest grade which, in the time-honoured phrase, was to be 'only attempted by experts'.

The self-confessed rabbit had suddenly acquired stripes. Moreover, the change occurred after he had suffered an horrendous wound that had taken away most of the bone between shoulder and elbow and left it joined together merely by splinters pinned to the remnants and an encasement of plaster. Despite this disadvantage, Dorothy Pilley in her mountain-eering memoir *Climbing Days* recalls that he indulged in 'most improper ventures'[3] for a man in his condition. Most particularly, a series of solo assaults on the Devil's Kitchen which, even in those days, had done little to shed its fearsome reputation. As Hamlet realised only too well, the choices when dealing with adversity are severely limited. Holland clearly decided to ignore the outrages of Fortune and chance his arm against this new sea of particular troubles. But my question is not that of the Prince of Denmark, but rather how and why did the change come about.

An obvious answer is that Holland, like many of us, was a man who learnt by hesitant degrees rather than in one continuous swoop of enlightenment. As the muscles need to rest after exertion so they can grow stronger, so may the psyche. It could have been a case of forward a bit, rest a bit, forward some more, and so on. The only problem with this theory is its lack of accord with Pilley's assessment of his climbing technique as one of those who 'prefer to go and do a new climb, without wasting time in airy speculation'.[3]

Alternatively, there may have been some significant event or events that caused this apparent change of attitude and Holland's involvement in the First World War might well have fitted the bill. The relatively flippant attitude we have already seen was continued in an article for the 1915 Fell and Rock Journal. This gentle lampooning of martial authority, ridiculous heroics and outrageous feminism was probably in line with the general attitude of the time—all a bit of a lark, over by Christmas—but when two years later he submitted his next piece, the tone had changed.

In 'Pictures in the Fire', his nostalgia for the 'dear, dead days'[4] is palpable. On the surface, it recalls his climbing before war broke out. In the flickering wraiths he saw winter struggles in the depths of Walker's Gully contrasting with sunlit slabs on Scafell's Pinnacle Face and the 'appalling ledge'[4] which he was so relieved to vacate in the early exploration of the Central Buttress of the same cliff. The bits that he found difficult despite constant practice. The bits that were difficult and found him dangling on the end of a rope. But, woven within the narrative, is his great admiration for Herford and the sense of loss at his death, and how that single event epitomised the author's unspoken but no less poignant juxtaposition of the meaningful struggles of climbing difficult rocks and the pointless carnage of war. The final sentence about his friend is particularly telling: 'May the memory of what he was be a stimulus and an incentive to those of us who are left to play the game both on the rocks and off them.'[4] Perhaps, in the end, he decided to accept his own challenge.

But there were still two more years to go. After enlisting in the 4th Battalion Gloucester Regiment, he was quickly nominated as officer material and in the fierce battle for Leipzig Redoubt in 1916 was awarded the Military Cross in recognition of his daring leadership. In 1917 he received the serious wound to his arm in a struggle where he received a bar to his MC. How much the memories of Wasdale with its climbs and climbing companions had sustained him, we can never tell, yet when he returned a new determination had emerged.

There is a thin line between determination and foolhardiness and, as his antics in the Kitchen had demonstrated, Holland was more often than not prepared to teeter on the edge of it. There is no better example than the first ascent of Holly Tree Wall in Cwm Idwal. This band of rock, although little more than 100 feet high, had long stood as a barrier between the easy routes on Idwal Slabs and the Continuation Wall above, a combination of which would allow 600 feet of continuous climbing. I A Richards, husband of Dorothy Pilley, had been on the first ascent of Hope in 1915 and had long cherished an ambition to solve the problem and complete the link.

The key, according to Richard's researches, was a holly tree perched halfway up the face. If this could be reached, the rock above appeared reasonably straightforward. The start was inauspicious. There were two points of attack but the easier was discarded as it seemed to lead to an impossible slab. So Richards set off up the second. It took an ice axe, a lassooed projection of rock and a good bit of pushing and shoving before the first man could reach a stance at the top of a series of corners. Holland then followed with help from above, but Pilley, even with Holland's assistance, was completely defeated. Richards then descended the discarded slab, which appeared somewhat less impossible after closer inspection, so enabling Pilley to climb the original choice and the whole party to regroup under the holly. All attempts to force the crack that lay above failed and their plans appeared thwarted. Holland, more in hope than expectation, made his way along a series of small holds to a point where he felt 'like a sparrow upon the housetops, though without the sparrow's advantages'.[5] After a precarious struggle he succeeded in reaching easier ground whence success was virtually ensured.

The party, however, was not satisfied. As it was unreasonable to expect following parties to equip themselves with an ice axe and the skills of a circus cowboy, they concluded the top had been reached, but no route had been climbed. They once more trooped to the foot of the cliff and eventually found and duly led Pilley's alternative start and the slab above, then, finally contented, made their way home.

They returned at a later date, when Richards found the crack behind the holly tree perfectly straightforward, and it is now generally agreed that Holland's variation is rather harder than the crack that caused so much trouble on the first ascent, offering proof, once more, that climbing is as much in the strength of the mind as in the power of the body.

The remainder of the summer was no less eventful. Only one other new route, Oblique Buttress on Glyder Fach, was added and then more by chance than design. After a particularly lively evening, Richards and Holland were in no mood for heroics and were probably seduced by the ridiculously easy first pitch. However, it was one of those climbs that gets progressively harder, reserving its final twist for the very last move before easier ground can be reached. Whether the delicate balance needed to execute the crux was a suitable cure for a hangover is not recorded.

Nor did the acrobatics stop there. The pair scoured the district, tackling much of what was on offer. It was during one of these outings that Holland's mountaineering career nearly came to an abrupt end. He had an unique climbing action, described by Pilley as 'crawl-and-pounce'.[3] As a result, the knees of his breeches needed constant refurbishment. Tired of paying the chambermaid of the Pen-y-Gwyrd Hotel half a crown a time, he instructed her to sew something more substantial beneath the torn remnants. This she did with a swatch of Axminster carpet. It proved more than fit for purpose and Holland was justifiably proud of his latest red and green accessory. It turned out, however, to have its limitations.

Running repairs effected, they returned to Lliwedd, with Central Chimney their main objective. Richards, who was leading, had a sudden and inexplicable lack of confidence and, but for a providential hold, would most certainly have taken a nasty tumble. Badly shaken, he retreated to the foot of the climb, safeguarded from above by Holland. The new leader then started to climb down to join his companion. What, however, he had not taken into account was the extra bulk of his newly equipped trousers. He jammed a knee in the crack in a manner that had, until this point, served him admirably. Now, in its latest fashion, it failed to hold and Holland joined Richards at the foot of the pitch rather more quickly than he had intended. Doubly shaken, they decided to set their sights on the easier target of Far East Cracks. Easier, that is, provided the softer options are taken.

With Holland leading, all went sufficiently well for him to suggest, rather than escaping to easier ground on the left, he should try the, much harder, Direct

Finish. All seemed to be proceeding in a satisfactory manner until Richards, to his consternation, noticed Holland was employing the self-same technique that had engineered his previous downfall. A toe-hold slipped, causing the padded knee to do likewise and leave the hapless climber scrabbling to regain some sort of purchase on the rock face. If, on previous occasions, he had tiptoed the aforementioned 'thin line', Holland's position was now very much *en pointe* and the inevitable happened. But, instead of a graceful slide as before, his exertions caused him to turn turtle and hurtle head-first towards his hapless second.

Richards, meanwhile, was busy assessing the situation. As his stance was inadequate and with his belay in danger of slipping from its resting place, he decided the wisest move was to wedge himself in the groove as best he could and catch Holland as he sailed past. As it takes little time for a body to fall fifty feet, the projectile arrived sooner than expected and Richards was only able to grab Holland's legs before he disappeared completely out of sight. The latter extricated himself from the tangle and at first seemed unperturbed by the incident, being more concerned about the state of his plastercast. After seeing to that and lighting a pipe, he even suggested that he should have another crack at it. Wiser councils prevailed.

Holland, in fact, advocated the virtues of falling off and advised all climbers to practise falling, or at least jumping, off rock faces onto boulder-strewn ground to improve their future chances of survival. This particular branch of callisthenics reached its climax the following year during a trip to Skye where Holland had already executed one of his impromptu sitting glissades down the slabs of a very wet Cioch Gully, which he later described as being a performance 'distinguished by ease and considerable grace'.[3] On the last day of the holiday, he and Dorothy Pilley were descending Shadbolt's Chimney on the Bhasteir Tooth. It is straightforward enough in ascent but Holland got himself all wrong while trying to effect a landing out of the fissure into King's Cave. Another backwards tumble ensued and Pilley found herself clinging onto the rope as her leader once more disappeared over the edge of, in this case, a 200-foot void. Holland takes up the tale:

After an abrupt descent through space I found myself hanging head downwards against the wall below, thus adding several feet to the climb. Although, theoretically, this unorthodox movement should have resulted in bodily damage, the contrary happened, for in bouncing on a ledge the last remaining adhesion left from a wound in the right arm was knocked out and the arm was afterwards considerably better from the shock. This falling movement, however ... is best left to the expert.[3]

If the summer spent with Richards and Pilley had begun the conversion from novice to expert, the following year, 1919, was its culmination. He had returned to the Lake District with a winter, and possibly a wartime, of planning in his head. He later wrote that, despite opinion to the contrary, he had always believed there were 'plenty of new climbs in the Wasdale district'[6] and it is now clear that he intended to put this theory to the test.

He had soloed a new climb on the Napes but you can tell from his dismissive assessment, 'a way of descent late in the evening',[6] that he had hatched bigger plans. The problem was to find the companions to match his ambition. So he was delighted to hear H M Kelly had changed his holiday arrangements and decided to spend some time at Wasdale instead. Holland had never met Kelly, so the latter was understandingly astonished to receive the somewhat imperious but now legendary telegram: 'Bring one pound of Capstan and two pairs of rubbers. Holland.'[7]

Harry Kelly was two years older than Holland but had not started climbing until he was thirty. Excused war service, he quickly established a name for himself on his local gritstone edges, but his first love was the Lake District where he produced nearly fifty new routes. A reserved individual (members of the Fell and Rock never discovered how he made his living) he was nevertheless the perfect foil for Holland's exuberance. Kelly wrote in the latter's obituary that his companion 'climbed with an élan which, complementary to my more sober approach to any rock problem, contributed, I am sure, to the success of our climbing partnership'.[7]

Holland wasted little time in putting his plans into action and on 28th July led Kelly up a new route on the West Wall of Steep Ghyll. Although other attempts on Scafell were to follow, including an abortive attempt of what was to become Moss Ghyll Grooves, Holland's main hopes lay elsewhere. The last stretch of significant unclimbed rock in the district was the west face of Pillar Rock, which was bounded to the north by Fred Botterill's North West Climb and to the south by Jordan Gully. John Atkinson had reached the top of the rock in 1826 by the Old West Route, which starts on the west face before moving onto the north, and it was three-quarters of a century before the Abraham brothers constructed the New West Climb to wind around the obvious difficulties in the centre of the face. In 1911 Hugh Pope climbed

100 new feet at the extreme south end of the face but was forced to finish up the New West.

So, when Holland and Kelly started their assault, there was only one climb that truly led from the bottom of the west face to the top of the Rock. A fortnight later there were five. The first of these was to give an independent finish to Pope's route. With Dorothy Pilley on 24th July, Holland had succeeded in creating an alternative to joining the New West but had been forced into Jordan Gully. Three days later, with Kelly's help, he finished the job. He next turned his attention to a continuous slab of rock that began at the foot of the groove on the New West, then stretched to the top of the crag. At first he thought it would be no more than an alternative and more attractive finish to the original route but later investigation revealed a separate rib of rock that ran to its base and, if combined, they would create an entirely new route. So, on 29th July, Holland led Kelly and C G Crawford up his discovery and the Rib and Slab was born.

But the obvious challenge, as with Scafell, was the central buttress. On 9th August, the final day of Kelly's holiday, he and Holland set off once more along the High Level and by the end of the day they had put up two entirely independent climbs on the West Face. The first was directly up the centre of the cliff, only deviating to avoid two overhangs, and the second was more to the left and, in Holland's view, even harder and probably not worth repeating. This view, however, may have been tempered not only by Holland being struck on the head by a stone and losing his precious pipe, but also by the state of his footwear. Despite the telegraphic call for reinforcements, the soles of both gymshoes had finally become detached from their uppers and could only be kept in place by the not so simple expedient of jerking the knee upwards, then quickly slapping his foot on the hold to keep the offending pieces of rubber in place. As we have seen, his attempt to get his own back by suggesting the routes should be christened Sodom and Gomorrah (not to be looked back upon) was squashed and he had to settle for nothing more vengeful than the disdainfully prosaic Routes 1 and 2.

It is not surprising that his climbing footwear had reached the state it was. Carr recalls three days with Holland a short time before Kelly's arrival. In that time they accomplished at least a score of climbs, mostly at the severer end of the range, on Scafell, Great Gable and Pillar, together with 'almost all the climbs then known around Buttermere'.[8] Even on the day of the flapping gymshoes, Kelly and he had ascended Savage Gully which, up to that point, had been the hardest climb on Pillar, swarmed down the Old West, then up Route 1 to make the first descent of Rib and Slab before the calamitous Route 2 was completed. These certainly were not the days when you yo-yoed around a roadside E7 for half an hour before returning to Kath's Kaff for a well-earned rest.

Such was the success the summer of that *annus mirabilis*, that Kelly and Holland vowed to spend the next year in the Lakes together. You would, therefore, expect the list of new climbs published in the Fell and Rock Journal to bristle with their combined names. Kelly's was there, particularly on Kern Knotts, but not coupled with Holland's. The latter was certainly around and Kelly later confirms 1920 as one of their 'golden days',[7] but the only recorded new routes were the Nook and Wall Climb on Pillar Low Man, coupled with some relatively minor variations on Scafell's Pinnacle. Surely they couldn't have fallen out?

But appearances are deceiving. Closer examination of 'Climbs Old and New' shows that they completed several important second ascents and a number of first descents, including the first intentional one of Walker's Gully. It must also be remembered that they came to climbing relatively late in life (Holland because of the war had only spent two seasons in the area) and there must have been scores of established climbs still prominent on their wish list. There would also be other members of the club staying in Wasdale and both would feel it their duty and pleasure to help friends and acquaintances enjoy their stay.

The following two years followed a similar pattern, except that each became involved in greater designs. The Committee had clearly decided that, to assist members and outsiders to identify the variety of new climbs in the District, some form of guidebook should be published. In the Journal of 1921 the following cryptic note appeared under the heading Pillar Rock: 'Rumour speaks of mysterious party using a graduated rope, and consisting of manager or Oberherrklettermeister (with pencil and notebook), chief guide, deputy guide, trusty second, and witty member of the party.'[9] The instigator was, not surprisingly, Kelly, but his later acknowledgements show that Holland was not one of the group. Again, he must have been around as two particular efforts were noted in the Journal, both of which possibly tell us something about the man. The first, with a Miss Rathbone, was a new route named Rowan Buttress, a rather undistinguished bit of rock in Langdale that did not even a merit a grade. Whatever his motive for this piece of pioneering, it could not have been to enhance his climbing reputation and was most likely named and recorded to please his companion. The second was a spot of chimney sweeping on Doe Crag to clear a rockfall in Intermediate Gully.

In addition, Holland was probably saving his money for more ambitious plans. First, there were two trips to the Dolomites of Sud-Tyrol and, after the success of the Pillar Rock guide, it was decided there should be another for Scafell, and that no one was better placed to be appointed editor than Holland. This and the exploration of easy climbs on the Pulpit Rock on Scafell Pike must have consumed most of his time and energy but there was one new route, Juniper Buttress on Gimmer, that is worthy of note. Not for the quality of the climb but for the young men who followed his lead. These were A S Pigott and Morley Wood who, five years later, became the first men to break into the fastness of Clogwyn Du'r Arddu and launch a new era of climbing in the British Isles.

So the man who had climbed with George Abraham and thus, by extension, with the incomparable O G Jones, been close friends with Herford and Kelly, the greatest climbers of their eras, now, uniquely, had links with the generation that would produce Colin Kirkus and Menlove Edwards and a further leap forward in standards. Perhaps, at last, he felt that of 'those who [were] left to play the game' he had just about done his share and no longer saw the necessity to risk his neck.

At least it seems that way. Four years were to pass before he reappeared in print with an account of a visit to Rosenlaui in the Bernese Oberland, the last of his ground-breaking exploits. Thereafter his stream of articles for a variety of climbing journals became more nostalgically reminiscent, and a better picture of the nature of the man was allowed to appear. He was always generous in praise of others, grateful for the opportunities they afforded and self-deprecating about his own part in the proceedings. But, as his impish sense of humour betrays, this was neither simple flattery nor feigned false modesty. And the old 'edge' was still there. Unlike many of his contemporaries, he was extremely tolerant of change and innovation, supporting the sensible use of pitons, opening up the membership of the Club and educating the young through the medium of outdoor pursuits.

Then even the writing started to dry up and when, in 1937, he was appointed Vice-President of the Fell and Rock it seemed a suitable valedictory tribute. If it had not been for the second outbreak of Teutonic belligerence, that probably would have been that, leaving a contented figure with his pipe and slippers staring once more at 'the pictures in the fire'. But Holland was not a man to resist a call to arms and so the forger's pen was wielded. It is unlikely this fooled the authorities but someone wangled him a position as Instructor with Frank Smythe's Commando Mountain Training School. A final piece, centred around North Wales and the Pembroke coast, appeared in characteristic manner, showering praise on the bravery of others while belittling his own efforts.

Very little seems to be known about his private life. Even Carr had 'never heard of any children to [his] marriage'.[8] Described as a 'short, stocky, sharp featured man, with a grin that reminded one of a famous gargoyle on Notre Dame and a laugh that became more and more Rabelaisian after the second or third pint',[8] Holland was clearly a good friend and excellent company. But if you are looking for a single example to demonstrate his characteristic blend of perversity, wit and loyalty, it was on his first visit to the Dolomites. The rest of the party were staring out of the hotel window in awe of the soaring limestone towers that rose before them. Holland, seeing this, immediately proposed a toast, not to the majesty of the Great Wall of the Langkofel, or even other great ranges that awaited exploration by members of his Club, but to the Slab and Notch, the easiest but, for him, the most revered climb on Pillar Rock.

Care in the Countryside

LAKE DISTRICT GOES UNDER THE HAMMER
National Debt halved at a stroke!
A business consortium, believed to represent a
wealthy group of Chinese industr...

Although the relocation of Dove Cottage, Hilltop Farm and Napes Needle to facilitate a Heritage Ramble around the mint-cake and duckponds of Britain's Greatest National Treasure might be unlikely, it is not beyond the bounds of possibility. It was not that long ago that the thought of the cream of English football teams being owned by a potential of oil sheiks, drug barons and pornographers would have been laughed out of court. Now, top clubs creak under the weight of financial manipulation. Recent suggestions, moreover, that the Greek government might sell off an Aegean island or two and British Sites of Special Scientific Interest should be placed in the basket of assets owned by the likes of Walmart would once have been a suitable subject for satire rather than serious political consideration. Today, in a world where long-term investment is scuppered by the desire for short-term profit, anything is possible.

We live at a time when the philosophy of cut-and-run economics prevails and there is little evidence that it will do other than continue. Eventually, those who, through either chance or choice, fail to board the bandwagon will be left to pick up the pieces. But before that happens the many, who take delight in the variety of scenery and opportunity the British countryside provides, should take stock of the situation. They should be wary of assuming that after access legislation all the problems are solved or, still worse, selfishly calculate that, like fossil fuels, what is left will see them out. The political agenda still exists and those who would prefer to keep what they perceive as their land free from general intrusion have already started to mount a counter-attack. As a group, they are well equipped. Money, position and influence make a formidable task force.

So who are these vested interests? Do they have a reasonable case for claiming particular rights when it comes to using the countryside for their own ends? They can be divided into three main categories, commercial, military and recreational, but matters are more confused than that. Between some there exists a crossover of interests and, at times, even a symbiotic relationship. The recreational walker is only too glad to use the commercial outlets of pub and chippie;

individuals take work behind the bars and counters of these establishments so they can afford to walk and climb in the area; the takings counted on Sunday morning compensate the hotel proprietor for the noise and hassle of Saturday night. In these cases they rub along together and might well be persuaded to understand and respect their respective needs.

Others are less easy bedfellows. Although the case for harvesting renewable energy is undeniable, the viability of wind farms is sufficiently dubious to outweigh the perceived damage done by planting immobile windmills on every skyline. Hydro-electricity is much more reliable but the volume of falling water required is necessarily found in the remote and rugged areas that the hill-goer so much enjoys. And unspoiled means a long way from the general debris of the large towns and cities that most need the power. The infrastructure of pylons and sub-stations necessary to carry the power to its destination (some 600 in the case of the proposed Beauly–Denny line) makes complaint against windmills seem paltry. What is obviously needed is a compact source of explosive power at the point of need, but the N word disturbs a generation which still conjures images of mushrooming clouds and animals born with an inappropriate number of limbs.

The problems are obvious, the solutions not so and when potential answers appear, the result is often compromised. First, by what is rather patronisingly referred to as 'The Big Picture' which clearly the individual will not be able to grasp. In another guise, this is also 'The National Interest' which bases its credibility on asking questions that have only one reasonable answer. Such inquiries as *Do you want to leave your country undefended or your taxes to go up?* clearly beg the question, yet can result in claims of a democratic mandate to render tracts of open countryside inaccessible, or truncate public services regardless of the actual need and consequence.

The reason why most individuals can't grasp The Big Picture is not because it's too puzzling but because they only have access to a limited number of the jigsaw pieces. As the smokescreen of National Interest may well conceal a number of 'special interests' at work, open access to all relevant material from the very outset is essential. Which brings us to another problem. While there is no doubt that, with the advent of Wikileaks and its like, establishment behaviour is now under scrutiny, it does not mean that the investigations searching for 'the truth' have the best of motives themselves. Too often the media today is moved more by a desire to embarrass than to reform and once the public has surfeited on the requisite amount of *schadenfreude*, the matter is forgotten and the status quo returns.

Yet let us suppose that a firm and disinterested form of arbitration could be found; the inherent difficulties soon become apparent. If, for example, we choose the grouse moor as a case study, we soon see there are a variety of specific interests at play and, moreover, looming in the background, a potentially over-riding general interest to take into account. Take first the specific commercial, recreational and local interests. The estates, to maximise their shoots, want minimal outside interference; the walkers, as a matter of principle, want unfettered access; the shooters demand their paid-for pleasure and the local inhabitants clamour for the self-sustainability that comes with employment and relative prosperity.

But even these straightforward divisions are not clear-cut. Each party can make a very reasonable case for itself and a coalition of minorities can lead to inequitable results. The Moorland Association trumpets the fact the estates employ more than 350 gamekeepers and provide local labour with around 42,500 hours of yearly contract work. Walkers can claim they use and therefore sustain the local amenities. Shooters, paying up to £4,000 a day per gun, can insist their pastime underpins the whole economy of the area. While locals could make the point that the villages' continued existence makes the other activities more viable. So how can one be weighed against another or any reasonable compromise be reached?

If something has to give, let us examine the validity of the walkers' expectations. As most grouse moors are wet and tussocky, the majority of walkers avoid them for better-trod parts. In a recent twelve-month period, I spent a couple of dozen days on the Durham and Northumberland moors and saw less than half a dozen individuals. If, in return for limited access, a few concessionary paths were maintained and a suitably blind eye turned to the odd enthusiast who feels compelled to tick off some undistinguished lump that appears in Bloggs' List of Hills beginning with Z, something approaching the best of most worlds could be reached.

Yet even if this multi-faceted dispute were resolved, another problem could rear its head. Putting aside any thoughts that the slaughter of wild animals for fun is wrong, or the general public has an inalienable right to wander at will across uncultivated land, there is still an important general interest that must be considered. Ground that is wet and tussocky holds rain rather than allowing it to stream off into the nearby rivers. The consequent slow yet regular release of water makes moorland an ideal location for the collection of water to furnish the country's domestic and industrial needs. But a shooting-estate needs to sustain the grouse population, so manages the land by burning back the heather and destroying the bracken. This, coupled with overgrazing, can lead to flash floods which not only renders water collection more difficult but can wreak havoc on the surrounding countryside. An outcome that rather outweighs any advantage otherwise claimed.

Moreover, the short-term fear of bridges being swept away and homes destroyed is not as disastrous as the long-term effects of altering the ecological structure of the land. It is generally agreed that much of Britain's moorland acts as a carbon sink and that this country has a disproportionate area of the world's waste disposal system. Biodiversity is a natural asset which is directly responsible for pollination, medical advance, fertile soil and clean air and water. The problem, currently estimated to be a loss of 150 species of flora and fauna every 24 hours, is arguably more important than the economic crisis and money spent now would be saved many-fold later. It would therefore appear that anything that sustains or improves the environment should take precedence over the parochial selfishness of individual parties.

But what happens if it turns out that supposed global interest is little more than a special interest in disguise, favouring a group with particular economic and political clout? If what is generally thought to be in the interest of all turns out to be a pernicious special interest? Take one of the more bizarre, but perhaps illuminating, suggestions for land management that has been proposed by the owners of the Alladale Estate, a remote piece of land that lies north of Inverness and contains much of interest for the hill-goer. The suggestion is to turn part of the land into a zoo and application has been made for the requisite planning permission and Zoo Licence. The arguments, no doubt supported by the relevant EU Directives, will probably include the need for re-wilding, i.e. reintroducing once native creatures, wolves, wild boar, etc, which will have the spin-off of creating a tourist attraction, with the subsequent benefit of more gainful employment and a cascading of wealth. The estate hopes, probably correctly, that as the areas to be enclosed are relatively small, the question of interfering with access will not enter the decision-making process.

At first sight, this seems to be a not unreasonable request and no doubt the applicants will stress that their proposal is a sensible and proper compromise between the demands of various parties. Closer examination, however, reveals more than the odd flaw. It was reported by the Mountaineering Council of Scotland that at a public meeting it was admitted the estate's long-term plan was to fence off the whole 23,000 acres and encourage its neighbours to do likewise. Like China's army invading Tibet in a succession of small and apparently insignificant steps, it is clear that the estate is playing the long game. Individual objectors eventually either lose interest or get used to an idea once considered outrageous, and applicants with time and money can afford to wait for any changes in personnel or shifts of political power which may favour their cause.

As a result, requests for planning permission often work in a devious way. Even if the current proposal is rejected by the appropriate committee of the Highland Council, it does not necessarily mean the matter is at an end. A well-established ploy is to request more than you really need, then, after intial rejection, return with fresh plans that offer the expendable in return for really desired gains. In the Alladale case, to appease the owners of local livestock, the applicants have graciously agreed to remove the proposal for wolves and replace it with one for European bison.

Not only does this make them appear sensitive to the needs of others but has introduced the zoological red herring as to whether the animal was ever a true native inhabitant of Scotland. Get enough smoke and mirrors into the act and often the core issues are left to founder by the wayside.

Perhaps the hoped-for reality is summed up by the owner of the estate, Paul Lister, son of the co-founder of the furniture chain MFI, who claims the structures he hopes to put in place will stand the test of time, According to an interview with *The Observer*, he sees guests who can afford the £3,000 per night to hire the Alladale Wilderness Lodge 'being able to relax in an outdoor Jacuzzi, sipping champagne … interrupted only by the call of the wild'. A wilderness comprising a zoo, electric fences and bubble baths? I am not sure that is what John Muir had in mind.

Those who wish to oppose these plans, and the MCofS certainly does, need to look carefully not only at the fine print of the application but any implications that can later be turned to the estate's advantage. One possibility—to ensure that the animals are safely secured—is that it might be deemed necessary to have an outer fence, or even series of fences, which, while not part of the original permission for change of use, will nevertheless restrict access to a further area of the estate. Strategically placed, these could even prove effective in discouraging access at large if, for example, it forced the walker to cross a swift-flowing river at a more dangerous point than otherwise would have been the case. The acquisition of 'ransom strips', where narrow stretches of land, relatively useless in themselves, can bar the way to more valuable assets, has long been a favourite of property speculators, and variants on this line of thought have already been adopted in England by farmers turning key sections of a right of way into slurry pits.

Whichever way you look at it, the solution to the difficulties surrounding care of the countryside is beyond orthodox regulatory methods. The problems are obvious, yet nothing much seems to be resolved. Individuals still insist on their right to drive over-powered cars and heat their houses so they can walk around in T-shirt and shorts. Large consortia employ tame scientists to argue for the results that suit them best and nations agree to amelioratory measures in principle but renege in practice. In short, top-down legislation, tempered by the thought of the next elec-tion or repayment for past favours, does not work. So let's consider the alternative of grass-roots up and, in particular, the role of the hill-goer and how he or she treats the countryside they enjoy at so little cost.

To start off with, there is a price, i.e. adopting a possibly inconvenient philosophy that applies both specifically to the hills and generally to the environment at large. The problem is not a new one. The 1929 handbook published by the Onward Rambling Club lists the following admonitions and advice to its members:

The perfect rambler thinks of others as well as himself. He thinks of the farmer and his stock and closes gates. He knows … litter does not improve the landscape. The price of a footpath is vigilance.

These rules nowadays seem self-evident enough and would generally be followed without question but their existence in print shows that, at the time, there was a need to establish a code of behaviour that would eventually become endemic. Today, the contribution must be much more than shutting gates and not dropping orange peel.

A good starting point would be a thorough bout of self-assessment. There is an argument that of all the blights on the landscape, walkers are the worst. But before the Angry Anorak Brigade fume at the detail, they should reappraise the whole situation and accept that it has no more or less an over-riding right to roam than Lord Game-Slaughterer has the prerogative to surround his land with barbed wire and armed gamekeepers. At the very least, they should realise that overuse or natural disaster can lead to severe damage which can only be remedied by making the ground in question a no-go area for the necessary length of time.

To ease the damage means that you have to spread the load and the first consideration should concern the Sponsored Walk. Too often these follow the same route, such as The Lyke Wake Walk or the Yorkshire Three Peaks, and the proponents for worthy causes tend to arrive mob-handed. The result—an ever widening trail of destruction. Its sudden popularity is not hard to explain as the dual satisfaction of helping a worthwhile cause and completing a physical challenge is obviously attractive. But why climbing mountains rather than jogging round the local park? Perhaps its very beginnings were founded in the Three Peaks Challenge, where participants attempted to reach the highest summits of Wales, England and Scotland within 24 hours. In those early days it was a relatively harmless activity, where success or failure depended more on the reliabilty and speed of the car than the stamina of the walkers, and the frequency of its happening was limited by the number of owners willing to thrash their vehicles around poorly surfaced country lanes.

This is no longer the case and while it is probably an exaggeration to suggest that every weekend a slew of charabancs empties its contents on the inhabitants of Borrowdale at two in the morning, it is now a common enough occurrence to be considered something of a nuisance. It would be churlish and patronising to suggest that volunteers should not do such things but, given that most participants rely on those with expert knowledge to complete such a course, and as these experts will come from the ranks of those who enjoy the hills and understand the problems of over-use, every effort could be made to spread the load. There is little point in supporting cancer research, if you are trampling to death the very ecology that might provide the solution.

Cynics might suggest that there is more than an element of selfishness attached to this suggestion and that it conceals little more than a desire to have the hills to myself or, at least, in the company of like-minded companions (and I must admit that, having left the peace and calm of Kingsdale to join the endless jostling stream of Bank Holiday weekenders on the ridge between Whernside and Ingleborough, my reactions were somewhat akin to those of a learner driver who had inadvertently strayed down the sliproad of a motorway). But, in reality, the opposite is true. A truly selfish response from discerning hill-goers would be to encourage the hordes to trudge along those paths now so worn that they consist of little but paving stones and scrappy plastic netting, while keeping the best bits for themselves.

In fact, the mention of motorways is not inappropriate as their use by hill-goers has produced another scourge of the countryside. Where once walking the hills was an unhurried pursuit involving a week's stay in the locality and travel by public transport, it is now compressed into as short a time as possible. A typical day is to fill up the car at the cheapest point of sale, buy food, etc, at the nearest supermarket, drive as near as possible to the desired summit/crag, complete the ascent and rush home for a celebratory pint in the local pub. Net result: an average 200-mile round trip, a further deepening of the carbon footprint and an undermining of any attempts to stimulate the local economy.

In fairness, the motorways *per se* are not to blame; they are only the carriers of the disease of Munroitis and its various mutations. When the business of collecting Scottish hills over 3,000 feet began, it was a leisurely process spread over a lifetime. Considerable free time, planning and determination was required to complete Munro's list and during the fifty years that followed the publishing of his tables, only eight could claim a full hand. In the half-century that followed, assisted by up-to-date maps, satellite navigation and step-by-step guides, the number increased exponentially and by 2009 several thousand claimed that they had completed the task. By far the most significant reason for this change of pace has to be improved road communications, with all the consequent carbon emissions. How about a pilot scheme that includes a toll for any non-essential westward bound traffic leaving the M6 between Junctions 34 and 41?

This ease of travel is coupled with the modern mind-set that likes to set aside a slot in life to complete a particular task. Knock off the Munros before collecting all the islands in the Caribbean while reading the list of The 50 Most Important Works of Literature Written in the English Language, compiled by The Sunday Poser. Such is the desire to cut all possible corners that when a mountain magazine asked its readers whether forest tracks should be opened up to public vehicular access to the foot of the hill, more than a quarter thought the idea was at least acceptable and probably ideal. Perhaps some entrepreneur might instigate a suitable helicopter service to complete the Tables in a long weekend.

What seems to have been lost in the rush to complete is the greater experience. To drive uphill as far as you can, climb the hill, then rush off to the next port of call certainly misses a point. Not that I am against the collection of Munros or Corbetts or Grahams or Wainwrights or what ever list Uncle Tom manages to cobble together. In fact, the encouragement of such activities is as good a way as any of spreading the load. But when the importance of the outcome disproportionately outweighs the pleasure of doing it, then the values we attach to the countryside can swerve from respect to condescension and, like the chancers of the first paragraph, we merely loot what we want from the experience, Then, when it is no longer fit for purpose, move onto the next wilderness. It is time we realised that it is not enough just to protect the environment. We must improve it. All hill-goers, to justify their claim of a right to roam, should actively contribute to the welfare of the environment they so much enjoy. In simple terms, after you've chucked your ten pennyworth in, which way does the balance fall?

The sceptic's reaction to such a proposal is: *What difference can I make when emerging nations are throwing up coal-fired power stations at a rate of knots?* An answer can be found in the singular response of

Rebecca Hosking, who was so distressed by the damage that plastic carriers had done to the albatross population that, on return to her home in Modbury, she persuaded the local retailers to ban such bags throughout the town. This success caught the public imagination and the supermarkets, anxious to milk public enthusiasm, fell over themselves to instigate a voluntary reduction in their use.

This mixture of motives meant the manufacture of plastic bags was reduced by 37,700 tonnes a year. The sort of statistic that invites an 'if placed end to end' comparison. If one person can change public perception on such a large scale, then a collective of walkers and climbers should be able to do likewise. Or, as Dr Elizabeth Cripps in her recent research at the University of Edinburgh more specifically concludes: 'Rather than give up on the idea of doing anything at all, because an isolated sacrifice would make no perceptible difference to a collective-level problem, individuals might have a *moral duty* [my italics]—if the problem is serious enough—to act to promote effective collective action.'

So, for a start, what can or should we do to help the mountain environment in Britain? The simplest way is to assist financially any of the institutions that have been constituted for that purpose. An obvious example is the John Muir Trust. This took its name and inspiration from the man who, again single-handedly, pioneered the idea of the National Park in the United States, and was formed to introduce a similar concept in the highlands of Scotland. It all started in the Knoydart peninsula, part of which was owned by a famous brewing family, and romantically known as the Whitbread Wilderness. Accompanied by photographs of twelve pointers silhouetted against the fading Celtic twilight, the Sunday heavies weighed in on the loss of the last great remote area of Britain. As a result, public imagination was caught and enough money was raised by the Trust to buy sufficient of the estate to guarantee that it would no longer suffer the threat of absentee landlords or the MOD training troops to yomp around the Falklands.

Many, probably, thought that was the end of the matter and returned to their BMWs thinking now all would be well. But it was soon realised that the solution of one problem revealed another. Unlike Yosemite, Scotland has no wilderness in the real sense. The Highlands are a place where people live and work. Only by giving control of the estate back to its inhabitants could it be said that the original and proper concept of the Trust and its supporters had been achieved. Although money is still necessary, voluntary labour to help to rebuild and maintain the estate is equally valuable and any Munroist who willingly suffers the monsoons and midges of north western Scotland is ideally equipped to put in a few hours on a regular basis. In fact, an ideal way to celebrate a completion of Munro's compilations would be to make a suitable donation to acknowledge the work that the Trust has done.

The second type of institution that deserves the hill walker's support is that which safeguards the existing rights of way. Although, in theory, in England and Wales these have to be maintained by the Highway Authority, economic shortfalls means that inertia is the norm. Once gone, they may be gone for ever and access to the open country could be denied. The following posting on the Government's *Your Freedom* website is instructive:

Repeal of section 130 of the Highways Act. This law is the bane of all landowners who have public rights of way on their land. It allows an individual who is very likely to be an extremist neighbour with an agenda to take action against local authorities ... [which] ends in some very questionable judgements which are often of no value.

I wonder whether the proposer of this solution would be equally happy if I suggested abolition of the law of trespass because of extremist landowners with an agenda? Landowners who rely on the law to justify their behaviour can hardly gainsay walkers desiring to exercise their own rights.

You can take an active part in safeguarding these rights. To become a Footpath Inspector for the likes of the Peak and Northern is a reasonable way to repay the hours of pleasure volunteers have ensured over the years. And, while on the subject of repayment, there can be few cheaper television programmes than having a suitable enthusiast lead the viewers through the Lake District or similar. After all, there can't be many shows where the star appears free of charge. Perhaps Auntie might consider a contribution from the Licence fee, or a bit of subtle propaganda on behalf of the Green party.

But, as already suggested, the most important contribution is how we behave as individuals. Using public transport, staying in the area and supporting local shops would benefit not only those immediately concerned but also, in terms of carbon emissions and food miles, the global community at large. We could be more selective when it comes to buying hill-going necessities. To take one example, it requires twelve litres of water to manufacture one litre of bottled water. A lightweight waterbottle should last a lifetime and be refilled without cost. Similarly, wear and tear of clothing and rucksacks can be mended rather than automatically thrown away and replaced by stuff shipped from the other side of the world.

Eventually it must come down to how we think about the hills and the way we deal with them. We must wean ourselves from the smash-and-grab mentality and develop a more sympathetic and considered approach. Learn to accept that you can offset the inconvenience of not using the car with the pleasures a different approach can bring. For a Munroist requiring to collect all the hills around Ben Alder, what better way than to leave a train at Dalwhinnie and, after a week exploring the area by sleeping at the bothies at Culra and Ben Alder Cottage, reboarding a train at Corrour for Fort William and a decent bath, with more than a dozen scalps in the bag? Or, by linking the bothies at Glen Beg and Knockdamph, complete a Trans-Scotia Expedition from Bonar Bridge on the east coast to Ullapool on the west, picking up en route such isolates as Seana Braigh and (in case you decide to move on to the Corbetts) Carn Ban. In fact, with a multi-journey rail pass and a judicious mixture of bothies, bivvies and better bed and breakfasts, you may well have a holiday that changes your perspective on the sunrise and sunset of your ambitions.

I have touched on these matters before but feel no need to apologise if the hand seems rather heavy. I would justify the weight by returning to the edicts of the Onward Rambling Club, where one further piece of advice is offered:

Respecting the rights of others he [the rambler] is able to resent the unjust taunt that he is the cause of rural disfigurement.

If, by 'resent', the writer means 'refute', he put his finger on the point more than eighty years ago. The implications of this observation, given the current floods and famine that are the result of global warming and mankind's selfishness, are even more true today. The post-war generation has, as Harold Macmillan remarked, 'never had it so good' and such good fortune demands some act of reciprocation. So, in this complicated game of Pass-the-Environmental-Parcel, we must do all we can to ensure that, at the final unwrapping, more is left than a desiccated husk.

A Conspiracy of Cartographers

I am not sure what sparked my interest in maps. It might have been books—the chart in *Treasure Island* or the endpapers that bound the secrets of Arthur Ransome's novels. But I suspect it probably happened rather earlier in what wasn't really a story book at all. In fact, it was more a book of drawings with very few words. On page one, there was an illustration of two children who appeared to be walking along a country lane to arrive at a crossroads. Here there was a signpost, arms pointing in each direction, with the instruction to choose one and move to the nominated page. Once the choice was made, their decision ended in one of two results. Either the chosen page showed another junction with a similar signpost or some impasse such as a broken bridge, in which case they would have to return to square one and choose a different road. This continued through a mixture of forks, T junctions and dead ends until, by trial and error and flicking backwards and forwards, they eventually reached the page that revealed the hidden treasure and journey's end.

Apart from its interest as a prototype for Game Boy or an early example of a post-modernist novel, the idea was intriguing in its own right. At a later point in the game, the reader could make an entirely different choice, only to arrive at a previously visited dead end—the same broken bridge, for example, but as seen from the opposite side of the river. Even more confusing was that, on one occasion of choice, you were being watched by a farm labourer leaning over a gate with an air of straw-chewing detachment, while on another, you could see only his back, no longer in the foreground but tucked away in the middle distance. Similarly, distinctive clumps of trees or buildings would reappear in different illustrations, either from a different perspective or in greater or less detail.

Although, essentially, this was a game of snakes and ladders, with guesses taking the place of dice, there was also an element of skill. The different perspectives suggested that some sort of overall plan was at work and, if the drawings had a greater purpose than mere illustration, the choices the reader faced need not necessarily be random. This suspicion was confirmed when, by either chance or design, the reader reached the page showing the elusive trove, and additionally found an instruction to turn to a page that showed a previously undisclosed map of the whole area, where the juxtaposition of all the roads, dead ends and accompanying furniture was revealed.

It was then that you realised (though I probably didn't at the time) that the conundrum was not only a game of winners and losers but also a sort of jig-saw puzzle that turned into a maze and, by comparison, Captain Flint's cartographic Pension Plan was little more than a thumbnail sketch. As I said, I probably didn't understand the implications at the time but, as with algebra and the distinction between the indicative and subjunctive moods, it might well have fermented in my brain until at last enlightenment dawned. I may add, an understanding of map dynamics proved to be considerably more useful than my early scholastic travails.

And what I certainly hadn't picked out of my child-hood reading was the power of these topographical representations. Maps, as Dr Sarah Bendall explains in her introduction to Jeremy Harwood's *To the Ends of the Earth*, had changed the world, in a variety of ways. Not so much for the obvious boost they gave to the exploration of unknown territories (even without maps, this would have been an inevitable if slower process) as the effect they had on social, political and economic history. Two examples will suffice.

In 1815, the culmination of a military campaign significantly changed the face of the world for the best part of a century and Wellington's cartographic enthusiasm played a major role in his victory. Such was his reliance on up-to-date maps for accurate intelligence, it even extended to a mobile printing press in his luggage. So, while he waited for Napoleon to attack, the Duke drew up and had mapped a number of potential sites for the eventual battle. Armed with copies, his Chiefs of Staff were able to deploy their forces in the most advantageous manner, regardless of whatever tactics the enemy might employ.

The consequences of the second piece of map-making would have been much harder to foresee, as a considerably longer period of gestation lay between the act and the outcome. In 1763, British surveyors, Charles Mason and Jeremiah Dixon were commissioned to settle a boundary dispute between two owners of property in, respectively, Pennsylvania and Maryland. The line they drew was eventually extended across the breadth of Pennsylvania, not only to separate it from Maryland but also from Virginia. The Mason-Dixon Line, as it came to be known, was seen, in the lead-up to the American Civil War, as representing the political boundary between the Union and the Confederacy and became a symbol for the dividing line between social freedom and human oppression. For many, it made a deal of difference which side of these particular tracks they were born.

Sadly, maps and attempts at oppression have often gone hand in hand. The study of geography rarely troubled my academic career but I can still quite vividly recall one lesson which took place at the primary stage of my schooling. A stoutly impressive lady produced a long bolt of paper which she proceeded to hang from a protuberance above the blackboard. There followed a ceremonial unrolling that systematically revealed a violent splash of colours, somewhat dominated by a regimented sweep of pillar-box red. She proudy presented each section of the Empire on which the sun never sets, accompanied by somewhat belittling references to the various blotches of blue, yellow and green that made up the imperial second division. I found the performance inexplicably dispiriting, but put it down to the appearance of the classroom which reminded me of the shelter in which we sought refuge from the wailing sirens and engine-droning that preceded the attempted destruction of the not so distant docks. And it would have been a wise child who could have connected the political bombast of Victorian cartographers with a similarly cartographic representation of *Ein Volk, Ein Reich, Ein Führer* commissioned by Hitler to justify Germany's attack on Czechoslovakia, Poland and beyond.

Fortunately, I was still in *Treasure Island* mode and

associated maps with a more innocent pleasure. My future archive was based on the discovery in a box-room of a stiff leather pouch designed to hold three one-inch maps, which in turn were supplemented by relics of spinster aunts' cycling holidays around the valleys of North Wales. Any further collection was a higgledy-piggledy affair but, through the process of beg and borrow, the space allotted on the bookshelf gradually expanded. I am not sure many of them had much use but that was scarcely the point. I found them interesting not for what they did, but for what they were. There was something therapeutic about opening up a map, spreading it out and smoothing the creases. Indeed, it is one of the delights of maps that they hide rather than flaunt their charms. Maps, tidily folded in well-bound books, pulled out to reveal plans of battle and voyages of discovery. Cleverly constructed relief maps popped up when the page was turned. Endpapers peered almost coyly around dust-jacket flaps. They all became constant companions accompanying my early reconnaissance and later reappraisal. Nowadays many are old friends, dog-eared with creaking joints and fading notes jotted in the margins, a shadow of their former selves that once refolded to lie as neat and crisp as a new deck of cards.

At first, my interest was indiscriminate, but after a while a pecking order arrived and the likes of *Boston and Spalding* sank into the more remote recesses of the bookcase. The maps that really held my attention had to show a preponderance of ever-deepening shades of brown or tightly packed contours and crinkly lines denoting cliffs and crags. It was for the latter reason that my original favourite was the two-and-a-half-inch-to-a-mile map of southern Borrowdale. It was also, at a later date, to prove extremely useful. From Newcastle it was almost as quick and certainly more productive to travel to Keswick than to some of the far-flung and little developed outcrops in Northumberland. On an early Sunday morning you could be west of the A6 in little more than an hour and making the first move on a sheltered Shepherds Crag before breakfast had been properly digested.

Long summer days allowed you to chase up the wriggle of rivers and streams that flowed from the south into Derwentwater and to reach the crags surrounding Great Gable, or even Scafell, without too much trouble. When time was shorter, we stayed in the valley. Originally Borrowdale was dismissed in the Fell and Rock Guide as having little to 'interest the enthusiastic climber' but, as Mike Thompson pointed out in his alternative guide of 1965, this was more the fault of the climber than the Dale and if the latter had to bear any of the blame, it was because it hid its secrets under mounds of foliage and vegetation. In the 1930s, Bentley Beetham unearthed, often literally, scores of new climbs on more than a dozen still unmolested crags. A second wave in the 50s and 60s, led by Pete Greenwood and Paul Ross, dramatically raised the bar of difficulty. Large faces of rock like Great End Crag and the north face of Goat Crag slowly emerged from the jungle, boasting routes of similar length and difficulty to the traditional climbing haunts.

But my map, true to form, served more than the utilitarian purpose of locating the plethora of rock; it also kindled my wider interest in the valley. The sudden realisation that the markings 'Plumbago Mine (Disused)' or 'Old Copper Mines' hinted at a lifestyle far removed from the picture-postcard images of the Lake District Tourist Board and led to my wondering what events had inspired Birkett's Leap, Joe Bank's Fold or Eddy Grave Stake. Place names that lie on the enlightened side of confusion, like Low Snab, Nitting Haws and Brund Fell, played across the mind. I felt there was a need to counter the derision heaped on Beetham's climbs in the public bar of the Dog and Gun and, while it has to be admitted that discovering the whereabouts of Frigga's Staircase or The Higher The Better depended on the length of the grass and the climber's patience, such climbs also had their place. They were part of the Dale's delight and I enjoyed, particularly in winter, poking around the hillsides trying to link Beetham's peregrinations in the hopes of finding an interesting way to Blea Tarn or Low White Stones. It was a sort of bouldering with a purpose and, along with the overground speleological investigations of Doves Nest and Columba's Gully, provided a nice complement to the sterner challenges of Scafell and Pillar Rock.

I have, on occasion, been asked to nominate my favourite map, my Desert Island extra so to speak. If forced to decide, I would limit myself within fairly narrow parameters. It would have to be part of Britain, remote, combining a mixture of hill and sea, and, above all, inspirational. Captain Cook, on discovering the Aboriginal maps, judged them of little purpose as they seemed to have neither an understandable scale nor proper orientation. What the explorer had not realised was they were maps of 'Dreamtime' before the World was created and the landmarks depicted, though actual, were symbolic of an understanding of life and inspired the basis of their social and cultural behaviour. As with the Aboriginal maps, my choice

ong the line of the Great Glen from Fort
Inverness.

his as his baseline, Roy, at first virtually
ed, plotted all the land north and west of
ern Uplands Fault. He, understandably,
local hostility and was greeted with sus-
rever he went but his real problem was a
n of hazardous terrain and treacherous
though it was surveying practice to be in
ring spring and summer and turn the find-
e finished product during the inclement
ths, this was not as easy as in more moder-
s anyone with any experience of Scottish
be only too aware, rain, sleet and even
mmonplace in July and August and, if the
ut and the wind were to drop, you have
the miraculous appearance of the ubiq-
e. Nevertheless, after five years of forced
es, laboriously hauling heavy equipment
went, the Survey of the Highlands was

inued with his work and mapped the
us producing an accurate cartographical
whole of Scotland, which in turn planted
the Ordnance Survey maps that exist
ere was still a long way to go before the

of OS Sheet 33 *Loch Alsh & Glen Shiel* is as important
for what it doesn't show as much as for what it does.

Beyond each of its four margins lies an area that
defines this map's existence. To the east, a line of forts,
William, Augustus and Inverness, that once defended
the Lowlands from Highland invasion, now stand
guard over the mountain treasures that lie beyond the
Great Glen. To the north, at point 839274, the A890
leaves the road to the Isles to weave its tortuous way
through the Torridon giants to Ullapool, the gateway
to the hills of Sutherland, where Suilven, Stac Pollaidh
and Ben Mor Coigach trip across the imagination. To
the west, the edges of Skye hint at rocky island spines
that plot their route over the Minch and Atlantic to
the isles of St Kilda. To the south, lies the god-given
railway from Fort William to Mallaig, where passengers rubbing the London sleeper from their eyes
realise they are no longer on the 7.45 commute from
Dorking to Victoria.

And within its bounds, it more than holds its own.
Maps to the north might proclaim Liathach and An
Teallach over Sgurr na Ciche and Ladhar Bheinn. The
brooding cliffs that line Glencoe might be reasonably
more impressive than the swoop from the Cluanie Inn
to Shiel Bridge. The mass of the Cairngorm more vast
than the fractured glens and ridges of Kintail. Others

may win the battles yet, in my view, Sheet 33 wins the war. No sea loch rivals Loch Hourn. There is no stravaig more varied than that from Glen Dessary across the rough bounds of Knoydart to Barrisdale and then to Inverie with, en route, the surprise view at Mam na Cloich Airde, the bothy at Sourlies and a return ferry to Mallaig. No coastal road more revealing than the one from Shiel Bridge to Glenelg, boasting brochs and otters at every twist and turn. For those wishing a final touch, blend in the genesis of the John Muir Trust with a drizzle of Jacobite nostalgia.

Not all will agree. Other Pelicans may cry, with some justification, from the wilderness of Cumbria and Snowdon. But, whatever your taste in maps, all must concur that until the invention of electronic toys and devices, there never was such a useful appliance that would fit so neatly into your pocket.

Yet, as with many things, we rarely consider the difficulties that were overcome or the labour involved to produce this state of cartographic convenience. I was certainly no exception and most of what follows is as a result of discovering Rachel Hewitt's *Map of a Nation*. This 'Biography of the Ordnance Survey' charts every aspect of its narrative from the beginnings to the present day. History is unfolded and spread before you. No detail is omitted, no sense

of proportion lost. It is, in
umph in its own right and
tion, recommend a compl

It all started, as innova
of blood. After the mass
of Cumberland ordered
Colonel David Watson,
of the road system that
Scotland. During this o
dawned upon Watson t
was a complete Military
he commissioned Willi
surveyed the former's fa
complete the task.

Unlike most existin
often more ornament
only to depict every t
rivers but also includ
mountainous ranges.
military use, it had
and points of poten
than decoration, wa
Cumberland's aim
to such an extent t
extinguished for eve
string of forts, co

that lay a
William to

Using
singlehand
the South
faced muc
picion whe
combinatio
weather. A
the field du
ings into th
winter mon
ate climes.
weather wil
snow are co
sun comes
to deal with
uitous midg
route march
wherever it
completed.

Roy cont
Lowlands, th
image of the
the seed of
today. But th

Landranger and Explorer were to grace the bookshops and internet. The Act of Union in 1707 had theoretically joined the countries of England and Scotland together, but, not for the last time, Edinburgh felt it was playing second fiddle to London. So, many Scots took great pride in Roy's Survey, which underlined the sense of Scotland as a nation in its own right. There was nothing approaching such a detailed account south of the Border, where it was generally agreed that both the East and West Indies were better charted than the Home Counties.

At first the English establishment did not react, considering the proper place for mapping was to depict property for the purpose of estate management or to provide a lavish display that flaunted wealth and influence. However, the advent of the Seven Years' War altered matters. The possibility of invasion sharpened the mind and Roy was appointed to survey and map the south coast, with a view to providing military intelligence for its proper defences. Given his Highland experience, Roy soon realised that, for a proper provision of national security, a survey of the whole country was necessary or, at the very least, an accurate map of the coastline. The suggestion was well received at first but, with prohibitive cost and the danger of invasion receding, his plan was shelved.

To make matters worse, cartographic interest shifted from the particular to the general. Rather than continue with their respective surveys, the energies of French and English surveyors were concentrated on determining the exact position of the lines of longitude and latitude. But, by chance, there was one spin-off that was to prove very useful to future hill-goers of Britain. In the early 1770s, the Astronomer Royal, Revd Nevil Maskelyne, decided to measure the size and shape of the Earth and, with the aid of Charles Mason (as of the famous Line) set out to find a symmetrical mountain around which he might conduct his experiments. His specification was pretty exacting: the hill had to be approximately half a mile high with the longer axis running east–west and, for the most part, with a surface free from hollows and bumps.

Eventually, after much searching, Mason came up with Schiehallion and Maskelyne set up camp on its summit. Although the survey drew a red herring across Roy's grand design, it did have two significant consequences for the map-making of Britain's mountainous areas. Mason's investigations meant he had to look at mountains from a different point of view. Rather than seeing them as hostile indefinite lumps, he had to consider each in its own light, how it stood separately and how it connected with the other hills around it. Second, in the process of measuring the density of the mountain, Maskelyne ordered the troops to place circles of chains around the hill to join points of equal height. The corresponding lines were then drawn on the map which were duly translated into the contours of today.

But the delay to mapping Britain as a whole was only temporary. Where military effort and civic enthusiasm had failed to put a national survey at the top of the agenda, wealth and political power succeeded. Charles Lennox, 3rd Duke of Richmond, coupling his lifelong interest in cartography and his duty to guard his portion of the south coast, decided to take up the cudgels. A long-time advocate of a thorough survey of England and Wales, he sensed the relationship between geography and military defence and, despite falling out with George III (not helped by his sponsorship of the contentious Reform Bill), he was eventually appointed to the post of Master-General of the Board of Ordnance, among whose duties was a responsibility for the undertaking of military surveys.

Once in post, and inspired by his earlier discussions with the now deceased Roy and renewed fears of a French invasion, he succeeded in reintroducing the 'Trigonometrical Operation' necessary to produce a National Survey. This, in effect, was a grid system which identifies every point on the ground with its mirror image on the map but, whereas it was adequate for scientific purposes, it was lacked sufficient detail to get an accurate picture of the ground. The military wanted to know the whereabouts of rivers that had to be crossed and the nature of any terrain that could give their troops a military advantage. To this end, it was decided to employ further groups of 'interior' surveyors who would reduce each original portion into a series of smaller squares, then, through closer examination, add the required flesh to the trigonometrical bones. To assist those who followed, the original survey left cairns of stones to mark their points of calculation. These 'trig points', changed to the familiar concrete pillars at the time of the Second Survey, have in due course proved a more than useful aid to generations of hill walkers.

So, in 1791, Ordnance Survey maps as we know them were born. Because of the threat of invasion, the southern coastal counties were the first to be inspected and once these had been completed the survey would sweep west and northwards through the remainder of England and Wales until the Scottish border was eventually reached. Given the rate that Roy, with little assistance, had completed the task in Scotland, Charles Lennox, along with the Ordnance Survey's

Assistant, Isaac Dalby, and its Directors, Edward Williams and William Mudge, could reasonably have assumed that the job in England would be finished somewhere around the turn of the century.

Yet, from the start, matters moved rather slowly. Strangers wandering around with equally strange instruments while taking copious notes were naturally regarded with suspicion. So, unsurprisingly, the locals were less than forthcoming with information that might lead to the taxation of their legitimate concerns and prosecution of the more dubious. Moreover, scare stories of French spies abounded and suspicion fell on any offcomer in the district. Brian Friel's play *Translations*, set in Ireland, gives a vivid insight into the sort of problems the locals can cause. These ranged from playful sabotage—moving the surveying poles when English backs were turned—through the difficulties of translating Eirean place names into English, to the downright hostility of a nation that assumed, with some historical justification, that the whole affair was part of a general policy of national subjugation.

So, progress was slower than imagined (it was not until 1870 that map 108 of south-west Northumberland was triumphantly borne to the printers) but the blame for this delay cannot be laid entirely at the door of the surveyors. Although Williams was something of a dilettante, Mudge quickly took over the reins and nearly worked himself to death, forsaking much personal pleasure. His assistant and eventual successor, Thomas Colby, eschewed existing roads or tracks and remarched his team as the crow flies through the Highland bog and heather. His pace was furious, on one occasion managing thirty-nine miles in a day, and in one continuous expedition lasting twenty-two days covering 586 miles. He even filled in the parts that Roy had ignored as too inhospitable, such as the Shetlands and Hebrides, only failing in an attempt to reach the highest point of Sgurr Dearg on Skye. It was consequently felt if even Colby couldn't get to the top of this eroded basalt pinnacle it must truly be Inaccessible.

In fact, the devil, as always, was in the detail. In a country where the linguistic tradition was as much oral as written, fixing an acceptably correct spelling for place names was never going to be easy, involving much searching in parish registers and the like. Matters scacely improved when the Welsh border was crossed. Not only were the onomasiological problems more complex, but the nature of the terrain demanded more hachuring than in the relative flatlands of England. This was a time-consuming method as all hills had to be depicted by a series of parallel lines drawn in black ink with the steepness denoted by their increasing density and darkness. Even when these problems were resolved, matters did not necessarily improve. The various departments, although united in a concerted effort, moved at different speeds and the whole procedure was accompanied by prolonged debates over the choice of scale.

At last all was done and the dignitaries could climb to the summit of Black Combe in the Lake District and in one sweep cast their eye over England, Wales, Ireland and Scotland in the sure knowledge that the Great Survey of the British Isles was complete. Since that date there have been visions and revisions and, as prices came down, an industry that catered for walker, cyclist and motorist alike. Metrication followed. Rights of Way were established and areas of public access clearly marked. In short, a complete collection for sack or shelf that would inspire and guide future generations. As with much of the publication that appears in paper form, their existence is threatened by satellite-based technology and the internet, but in my opinion the breadth of vision offered by an unfolded map far outweighs the narrow and somewhat parsimonious accuracy of the GPS.

A full understanding of all the twists and turns is to be found in Hewitt's book, of which the above paragraphs are but a rough summary. Although essentially a scholarly book (the Notes and Acknowledgements run to more than 100 pages), it is an entertaining read with a strong narrative line. There are two of her stories that I particularly liked. The first concerns the aftermath of the Schiehallion affair.

Unfortunately, the mountain lived up to its Gaelic name of 'Constant Storm' and for many nights clouds obscured the sky, making any calculation impossible. As a result, Maskelyne had to spend a good deal of time on the hill. Unlike Roy, however, the astronomer found the natives friendly. He enjoyed their regular visits to his makeshift bothy, often accompanied by the fiddle-playing of Duncan Robertson. At the end of his survey and as a reward for their efforts, he threw a party which became sufficiently boisterous to burn down the hut that housed it. The calculations were saved, but the fiddle was destroyed in the conflagration. Young Duncan was understandably heartbroken at the loss of his precious instrument, but was no doubt more than happy when Maskelyne, by way of compensation, sent him a Stradivarius.

The other occurred during the survey of southwest England but could easily have found its way into Brian Friel's Irish play. A zealous government official, acting on information received, reported of OS Sheet 33 *Loch Alsh & Glen Shiel* is as important for what it doesn't show as much as for what it does.

Beyond each of its four margins lies an area that defines this map's existence. To the east, a line of forts, William, Augustus and Inverness, that once defended the Lowlands from Highland invasion, now stand guard over the mountain treasures that lie beyond the Great Glen. To the north, at point 839274, the A890 leaves the road to the Isles to weave its tortuous way through the Torridon giants to Ullapool, the gateway to the hills of Sutherland, where Suilven, Stac Pollaidh and Ben Mor Coigach trip across the imagination. To the west, the edges of Skye hint at rocky island spines that plot their route over the Minch and Atlantic to the isles of St Kilda. To the south, lies the god-given railway from Fort William to Mallaig, where passengers rubbing the London sleeper from their eyes realise they are no longer on the 7.45 commute from Dorking to Victoria.

And within its bounds, it more than holds its own. Maps to the north might proclaim Liathach and An Teallach over Sgurr na Ciche and Ladhar Bheinn. The brooding cliffs that line Glencoe might be reasonably more impressive than the swoop from the Cluanie Inn to Shiel Bridge. The mass of the Cairngorm more vast than the fractured glens and ridges of Kintail. Others may win the battles yet, in my view, Sheet 33 wins the war. No sea loch rivals Loch Hourn. There is no stravaig more varied than that from Glen Dessary across the rough bounds of Knoydart to Barrisdale and then to Inverie with, en route, the surprise view at Mam na Cloich Airde, the bothy at Sourlies and a return ferry to Mallaig. No coastal road more revealing than the one from Shiel Bridge to Glenelg, boasting brochs and otters at every twist and turn. For those wishing a final touch, blend in the genesis of the John Muir Trust with a drizzle of Jacobite nostalgia.

Not all will agree. Other Pelicans may cry, with some justification, from the wilderness of Cumbria and Snowdon. But, whatever your taste in maps, all must concur that until the invention of electronic toys and devices, there never was such a useful appliance that would fit so neatly into your pocket.

Yet, as with many things, we rarely consider the difficulties that were overcome or the labour involved to produce this state of cartographic convenience. I was certainly no exception and most of what follows is as a result of discovering Rachel Hewitt's *Map of a Nation*. This 'Biography of the Ordnance Survey' charts every aspect of its narrative from the beginnings to the present day. History is unfolded and spread before you. No detail is omitted, no sense of proportion lost. It is, in fact, a cartographical triumph in its own right and I would, without reservation, recommend a complete reading.

It all started, as innovations so often do, in a field of blood. After the massacre at Culloden, the Duke of Cumberland ordered his General Quartermaster, Colonel David Watson, to supervise an extension of the road system that led into the Highlands of Scotland. During this operation, it must have slowly dawned upon Watson that what was really necessary was a complete Military Survey of the Highlands and he commissioned William Roy, who had successfully surveyed the former's family estates in Lanarkshire, to complete the task.

Unlike most existing maps in Britain, which were often more ornament than use, Roy's map was not only to depict every twist and turn of the roads and rivers but also include a full survey of the glens and mountainous ranges. As this was to be a map for military use, it had to show existing lines of supply and points of potential ambush. So accuracy, rather than decoration, was the order of the day. For it was Cumberland's aim to destroy the Highland Clans to such an extent that the Jacobite threat would be extinguished for ever. The key to this venture was that string of forts, constructed after the '15 rebellion, that lay along the line of the Great Glen from Fort William to Inverness.

Using this as his baseline, Roy, at first virtually singlehanded, plotted all the land north and west of the Southern Uplands Fault. He, understandably, faced much local hostility and was greeted with suspicion wherever he went but his real problem was a combination of hazardous terrain and treacherous weather. Although it was surveying practice to be in the field during spring and summer and turn the findings into the finished product during the inclement winter months, this was not as easy as in more moderate climes. As anyone with any experience of Scottish weather will be only too aware, rain, sleet and even snow are commonplace in July and August and, if the sun comes out and the wind were to drop, you have to deal with the miraculous appearance of the ubiquitous midge. Nevertheless, after five years of forced route marches, laboriously hauling heavy equipment wherever it went, the Survey of the Highlands was completed.

Roy continued with his work and mapped the Lowlands, thus producing an accurate cartographical image of the whole of Scotland, which in turn planted the seed of the Ordnance Survey maps that exist today. But there was still a long way to go before the

Landranger and Explorer were to grace the bookshops and internet. The Act of Union in 1707 had theoretically joined the countries of England and Scotland together, but, not for the last time, Edinburgh felt it was playing second fiddle to London. So, many Scots took great pride in Roy's Survey, which underlined the sense of Scotland as a nation in its own right. There was nothing approaching such a detailed account south of the Border, where it was generally agreed that both the East and West Indies were better charted than the Home Counties.

At first the English establishment did not react, considering the proper place for mapping was to depict property for the purpose of estate management or to provide a lavish display that flaunted wealth and influence. However, the advent of the Seven Years' War altered matters. The possibility of invasion sharpened the mind and Roy was appointed to survey and map the south coast, with a view to providing military intelligence for its proper defences. Given his Highland experience, Roy soon realised that, for a proper provision of national security, a survey of the whole country was necessary or, at the very least, an accurate map of the coastline. The suggestion was well received at first but, with prohibitive cost and the danger of invasion receding, his plan was shelved.

To make matters worse, cartographic interest shifted from the particular to the general. Rather than continue with their respective surveys, the energies of French and English surveyors were concentrated on determining the exact position of the lines of longitude and latitude. But, by chance, there was one spin-off that was to prove very useful to future hill-goers of Britain. In the early 1770s, the Astronomer Royal, Revd Nevil Maskelyne, decided to measure the size and shape of the Earth and, with the aid of Charles Mason (as of the famous Line) set out to find a symmetrical mountain around which he might conduct his experiments. His specification was pretty exacting: the hill had to be approximately half a mile high with the longer axis running east–west and, for the most part, with a surface free from hollows and bumps.

Eventually, after much searching, Mason came up with Schiehallion and Maskelyne set up camp on its summit. Although the survey drew a red herring across Roy's grand design, it did have two significant consequences for the map-making of Britain's mountainous areas. Mason's investigations meant he had to look at mountains from a different point of view. Rather than seeing them as hostile indefinite lumps, he had to consider each in its own light, how it stood separately and how it connected with the other hills around it. Second, in the process of measuring the density of the mountain, Maskelyne ordered the troops to place circles of chains around the hill to join points of equal height. The corresponding lines were then drawn on the map which were duly translated into the contours of today.

But the delay to mapping Britain as a whole was only temporary. Where military effort and civic enthusiasm had failed to put a national survey at the top of the agenda, wealth and political power succeeded. Charles Lennox, 3rd Duke of Richmond, coupling his lifelong interest in cartography and his duty to guard his portion of the south coast, decided to take up the cudgels. A long-time advocate of a thorough survey of England and Wales, he sensed the relationship between geography and military defence and, despite falling out with George III (not helped by his sponsorship of the contentious Reform Bill), he was eventually appointed to the post of Master-General of the Board of Ordnance, among whose duties was a responsibility for the undertaking of military surveys.

Once in post, and inspired by his earlier discussions with the now deceased Roy and renewed fears of a French invasion, he succeeded in reintroducing the 'Trigonometrical Operation' necessary to produce a National Survey. This, in effect, was a grid system which identifies every point on the ground with its mirror image on the map but, whereas it was adequate for scientific purposes, it was lacked sufficient detail to get an accurate picture of the ground. The military wanted to know the whereabouts of rivers that had to be crossed and the nature of any terrain that could give their troops a military advantage. To this end, it was decided to employ further groups of 'interior' surveyors who would reduce each original portion into a series of smaller squares, then, through closer examination, add the required flesh to the trigonometrical bones. To assist those who followed, the original survey left cairns of stones to mark their points of calculation. These 'trig points', changed to the familiar concrete pillars at the time of the Second Survey, have in due course proved a more than useful aid to generations of hill walkers.

So, in 1791, Ordnance Survey maps as we know them were born. Because of the threat of invasion, the southern coastal counties were the first to be inspected and once these had been completed the survey would sweep west and northwards through the remainder of England and Wales until the Scottish border was eventually reached. Given the rate that Roy, with little assistance, had completed the task in Scotland, Charles Lennox, along with the Ordnance Survey's

Assistant, Isaac Dalby, and its Directors, Edward Williams and William Mudge, could reasonably have assumed that the job in England would be finished somewhere around the turn of the century.

Yet, from the start, matters moved rather slowly. Strangers wandering around with equally strange instruments while taking copious notes were naturally regarded with suspicion. So, unsurprisingly, the locals were less than forthcoming with information that might lead to the taxation of their legitimate concerns and prosecution of the more dubious. Moreover, scare stories of French spies abounded and suspicion fell on any offcomer in the district. Brian Friel's play *Translations*, set in Ireland, gives a vivid insight into the sort of problems the locals can cause. These ranged from playful sabotage—moving the surveying poles when English backs were turned—through the difficulties of translating Eirean place names into English, to the downright hostility of a nation that assumed, with some historical justification, that the whole affair was part of a general policy of national subjugation.

So, progress was slower than imagined (it was not until 1870 that map 108 of south-west Northumberland was triumphantly borne to the printers) but the blame for this delay cannot be laid entirely at the door of the surveyors. Although Williams was something of a dilettante, Mudge quickly took over the reins and nearly worked himself to death, forsaking much personal pleasure. His assistant and eventual successor, Thomas Colby, eschewed existing roads or tracks and remarched his team as the crow flies through the Highland bog and heather. His pace was furious, on one occasion managing thirty-nine miles in a day, and in one continuous expedition lasting twenty-two days covering 586 miles. He even filled in the parts that Roy had ignored as too inhospitable, such as the Shetlands and Hebrides, only failing in an attempt to reach the highest point of Sgurr Dearg on Skye. It was consequently felt if even Colby couldn't get to the top of this eroded basalt pinnacle it must truly be Inaccessible.

In fact, the devil, as always, was in the detail. In a country where the linguistic tradition was as much oral as written, fixing an acceptably correct spelling for place names was never going to be easy, involving much searching in parish registers and the like. Matters scacely improved when the Welsh border was crossed. Not only were the onomasiological problems more complex, but the nature of the terrain demanded more hachuring than in the relative flatlands of England. This was a time-consuming method as all hills had to be depicted by a series of parallel lines drawn in black ink with the steepness denoted by their increasing density and darkness. Even when these problems were resolved, matters did not necessarily improve. The various departments, although united in a concerted effort, moved at different speeds and the whole procedure was accompanied by prolonged debates over the choice of scale.

At last all was done and the dignitaries could climb to the summit of Black Combe in the Lake District and in one sweep cast their eye over England, Wales, Ireland and Scotland in the sure knowledge that the Great Survey of the British Isles was complete. Since that date there have been visions and revisions and, as prices came down, an industry that catered for walker, cyclist and motorist alike. Metrication followed. Rights of Way were established and areas of public access clearly marked. In short, a complete collection for sack or shelf that would inspire and guide future generations. As with much of the publication that appears in paper form, their existence is threatened by satellite-based technology and the internet, but in my opinion the breadth of vision offered by an unfolded map far outweighs the narrow and somewhat parsimonious accuracy of the GPS.

A full understanding of all the twists and turns is to be found in Hewitt's book, of which the above paragraphs are but a rough summary. Although essentially a scholarly book (the Notes and Acknowledgements run to more than 100 pages), it is an entertaining read with a strong narrative line. There are two of her stories that I particularly liked. The first concerns the aftermath of the Schiehallion affair.

Unfortunately, the mountain lived up to its Gaelic name of 'Constant Storm' and for many nights clouds obscured the sky, making any calculation impossible. As a result, Maskelyne had to spend a good deal of time on the hill. Unlike Roy, however, the astronomer found the natives friendly. He enjoyed their regular visits to his makeshift bothy, often accompanied by the fiddle-playing of Duncan Robertson. At the end of his survey and as a reward for their efforts, he threw a party which became sufficiently boisterous to burn down the hut that housed it. The calculations were saved, but the fiddle was destroyed in the conflagration. Young Duncan was understandably heartbroken at the loss of his precious instrument, but was no doubt more than happy when Maskelyne, by way of compensation, sent him a Stradivarius.

The other occurred during the survey of southwest England but could easily have found its way into Brian Friel's Irish play. A zealous government official, acting on information received, reported the presence of two individuals on and around the Quantocks, carrying charts and taking measurements while talking in an unintelligible gabble, presumably French. After further investigation, it was found that the 'spies' were no lesser persons than the poets Wordsworth and Coleridge who were studying the topographical detail for one of the latter's poems and the 'French', it turned out, was a heated conversation on the relative merits of Spinoza.

Re-reading all this, it struck me that my attachment to maps might be likened to that of a child to its security blanket, and there is no doubt there have been times when the analogy seemed particularly apt. On those occasions when I was confident I didn't need to take a map—only to find that I did. The time when I inadvertently lost my compass on the far side of nowhere and Landranger 42, despite my dithering, managed to bully me off the hill, out of the mist and back for the last train. The moment, in a whiteout, when the map said turn right when my better judgement inclined to the left over a precipice. Maps are important to me and, I suspect, to anyone else who loves hills. And one thing's for sure. If you come across some bloke wandering rather aimlessly in the wilderness without one, he is either an explorer, a cartographer or lost.

Bivouacs, Bothies & Rather Better Breakfasts

There are three types of accommodation—Basic, Standard and De Luxe—and these are paired, each according to its lot, with the Have-nots, Haves and Have-a-lots. Euphemisms such as 'economy' or 'bargain' draw the scantiest of veils over the truth that 'basic' means cheap, and cheap means no extras. The low-water mark of such frugality is where you have to hire the plug before you can take a bath. 'Standard' comes with extras, but you have to pay for them and the feeling of moral superiority associated with 'de luxe' is occasionally tempered by an inclination to steal the towels to offset the cost. As with hotels, so with life. Polo/Cricket/Cross Country Running; Café Royale/Little Chef/Pete's Eats; Manchester United/ Blackburn Rovers/Bury—the names may change but the principle seems to hold firm.

One would, therefore, assume that the title of this chapter indicates a similar progressive scale of desirability. But those who climb hills, of whatever size or by whatever means, appear to have their own set of values. To the world at large, the options of walking/driving/flying would underline the ascending progress of civilised man but, to the mountaineer, the opposite is true. To reach the summit using your own limbs is a triumph, in a 4x4 is a cheat and by helicopter a disgrace. Similarly, when it comes to overnight arrangements, the absence of luxury is not necessarily a bad thing. So, in any debate on the refuge of choice, there will always be those who swear by their separate relative merits. To one, the risks of discomfort are more than offset by the opportunity to see a secret world denied to lie-a-beds. To another, the pleasures of consorting with like-minded souls, a wood fire and a pair of dry socks are sufficient to forego a spring mattress. While to a third, the prospect of quail and venison accompanied by a half-bottle of claret is irresistible. My own inclination is towards a commissarial pot-pourri, where each weakness is compensated by the alternate pleasure it brings.

Of the particular advantages of bivouacking I have written elsewhere and, apart from one further observation, can do little other than recommend Ronald Turnbull's *The Book of the Bivvy*. It explains the dos and don'ts and whys and why-nots of the art, is inspirational in its suggestions and entertaining to read. My own contribution is on making the most of your holiday. It is often the case that, if you live in England, to get home from the Highlands is the best part of a day's travel and thus a day wasted. But if the evening before, having fed and watered, you bed down on the hill, you can easily be on the summit while others are wading their way through bacon and egg. This is especially useful if you are suffering one of the various strains of collectivitis and you need to whip in the odd isolate or tick off a summit you should have done en route, had not the pull of gravity towards the pub proved stronger.

I can remember two such last-minute outings that proved particularly profitable. The first was Meall Buidhe in Glen Lyon. It is possible, given reasonable conditions, to combine this summit with Stuchd an Lochain, starting and finishing at the dam of Loch an Daimh, but the route is 20km long and involves a steep up and down between the two peaks. On my first visit, deep soft snow prevailed and I had to be content with a laborious ascent of the Stuchd. This, rather annoyingly, left the Yellow Hill for another day.

The following year I decided to undertake a bit of a grand tour of the Highlands, starting with a sleeper to Fort William, then train to Mallaig, ferry up the Sound of Sleat to Kyle (a must voyage that follows the best and probably most remote coastline in Scotland) and finishing at Inverness via Plockton, Achnashellach and Garve. At various points I disembarked, gathering, in my case, Munros in May.

The final leg home was broken at Blair Atholl, where I had arranged to meet a friend for a day on the hills between Loch Lyon and Loch Rannoch. My original plan had been to return to the main line and continue south when I suddenly remembered the errant Meall Buidhe. If, after suitable refreshment, I could be dropped off at the right part of Rannoch Moor, I could bivvy on the flanks of the elusive top, execute a quick up and down at daybreak, and catch the first train to Glasgow from Rannoch Station. John and the weather duly obliged. On the second occasion, I spent a similar night outwith Corrour Station to complete a dawn raid on Beinn a' Bhric and Leum Uilleim, though why and from what William chose to leap proved a mystery I have yet to solve.

Both bivvies were really as good as they come— a sheltered hollow on dry springy heather, a softly running burn to induce sleep and act as the gentlest of alarm calls, an ever-deepening gloaming through which to savour the fading hills and final dram. There is something about lying close to the ground. Perhaps, like swimming in the sea, it awakens ancient memories. John Muir, the philosopher and proto-ecologist, used, during his geological investigations, to lie on his back to feel the movement of the earth beneath him. The official academics dismissed his theories as the aimless meanderings of an 'ambitious shepherd' but in the end he was proved right. The Yosemite valley had indeed been formed by a gentle glaciation rather than the accepted seismic faulting.

The memories of these final hours of my 'tour' remain only as a clutch of broken images, dawn breaking through swiftly dispersing mists, the ever-warming air and steady exercise massaging any stiffness from aching bones, a steady jog down the final ridge to sit in the sun on the station platform. The train arrives, stations roll by—Rannoch, Bridge of Orchy, Tyndrum, Crianlarich—breakfast courtesy of Scottish Rail. What price now the Hotel Splendide? Mind you, there was the night halfway up the hill above Achnashellach and the sorry flight to Gerry's Hostel. But that's another story.

The obvious advantage of a bivvy over a hotel is that you can start the day from wherever it suits you best and finish it whenever you have had enough. In terms of such overnight accommodation, the bothy is the halfway house. The open shelters at Ben Alder Cottage or Sourlies in Knoydart, apart from being a delightful experience in themselves, put a big day on the hills right on your doorstep. A much more attractive alternative than the long there and back haul from the stations at Rannoch or Glenfinnan.

Cottages of this type are nowadays maintained by the Mountain Bothies Association and are used by walkers, climbers and other outdoor enthusiasts alike. But a century or so ago they were family homes that supported a scattered population of crofters, shepherds and stalkers. Yet, even then, these relatively humble dwellings played a crucial part in the exploration of the Highlands. Sir Hugh Munro and his colleagues from the SMC would have counted on their hospitality to complete their long stravaigs and were, no doubt, welcomed as visitors bringing news from the outside world, particularly if there was a bottle of the 'water of life' hidden at the bottom of the rucksack. The story of Shenavall, on the Dundonnell Estate, gives an insight into how things were.

If you are going to move into a new house, then November in the north west of Scotland would not be the time and place of choice. But it was at such a moment in 1891 that Colin MacDonald and his family was transported by rowing boat to the head of Loch na Sealga. As they approached, the ring of the stonemason's hammer was still echoing across the water and when they arrived they were faced with no more than a stone shell standing on a bare earth floor. The sight would scarcely have inspired John Howard

Payne's immortal words on the benefits of domestic dulcification.

They plastered the walls with clay and wintered the best they could. By the end of next spring, upstairs bedrooms had been added, flooring laid and the inside walls wood-panelled. The project expanded and soon cows were producing dairy products, wool from the sheep was spun and a walled garden provided fresh vegetables. With venison and trout at hand and luxuries such as tea and sugar supplied by the Estate, they could now follow the self-sufficient pattern of life long practised by their scattered neighbours.

Not that life was all roses round the doorway. The weather can be unforgiving and in the winter of 1895-6 Shenavall was cut off between Christmas and the end of March, with temperatures so low that the whole of the loch froze over to the depth of several feet. In April, the thermometer finally rose but still much snow and ice remained. One morning a violent explosion, sounding like the Final Crack of Doom, was heard the length of Destitution Road. The thaw had freed the water under the ice to drain into the Gruinard River, leaving the frozen lake suspended like a giant ceiling. Eventually the weight grew too great and it collapsed, riven by an jagged crack six miles long.

These details of his life appeared in the 1990 Journal of the Mountain Bothies Association, as told by MacDonald himself to Alex Sutherland, a former President of the Inverness Mountaineering Club. Though still capable of a day on the hill, the crofter by this time was living in Dollar and the cottage, now abandoned, was being regularly used as an overnight refuge. Mountain writers from Bill Murray to Hamish Brown have extolled its merits and even the Heir Apparent has spent a night within its walls. There is no doubt that, as bothies go, it rates very highly and, with a backdrop of Beinn Dearg Mor sweeping into Loch na Seagla and An Teallach nudging the peripheral vision over your right shoulder, it is certainly one of the most photographed.

My own experience, although equally memorable, was not so idyllic. We had taken a group of experienced sixth formers to stay at Achnashellach, with a view to climbing the hills in the Torridon area. The centrepiece of the week was a three-day expedition across the ground that lies between Kinlochewe and Dundonnell, with overnight stops in the bothies at Carnmore and Shenavall. Although a small enough group, we were conscious of the need not to over-crowd the bothies, so split the party into two. Group A would start at Kinlochewe, climb Slioch and sleep at Carnmore. Group B would traverse An Teallach to stop over at Shenavall. On Day 2 the two groups would meet at an agreed point and, depending on the weather, spend the day together exploring the remote peaks at the west end of the Letterewe Forest before exchanging overnight accommodation. On Day 3 each group would walk out, completing its remaining summit.

In theory, the plan seemed feasible, although there were two obvious possible snags. As we were a long way from our base at Achnashellach, we would need to leave transport at each end of the crossing for the other group to pick up. We had two vans but only one set of keys per vehicle which we would have to swap when we met on Day 2. The second potential problem was that we might arrive at the bothies and find them to be full. This seemed unlikely, as Carnmore was very remote and little used and Shenavall, although popular, had six rooms on two floors. It was an ambitious programme but the group was pretty fit and, as it was midsummer, there was virtually unlimited daylight with few alternative distractions. If you can't get excited about the thought of Slioch, A'Mhaighdean and An Teallach in one fell swoop, then you may as well take up tiddly-winks or golf, or some other game that involves getting a relatively small object somewhere near the aperture of a slightly larger one.

Having satisfied ourselves that we had done our best to cover all corners, we set off. But, embedded in the paragraph before last is the seemingly innocent phrase 'depending on the weather', and to describe our weather as wet is to push the art of understatement into the realms of fiction. My group arrived at Dundonnell in a storm that threatened to tear the roof off the van. After an hour or so, the wind slackened and we made a start up the side of Bidean a' Ghlas Thuill, but at 1,000 feet the temperature dropped and the rain turned to sleet and the only sensible solution was to return to Dundonell and take the low level route to Shenavall.

It was a major disappointment (it was the third time that the weather had won the day in my attempts at An Teallach) but as we approached the bothy, the storm blew through and a watery sun encouraged the belief that we might yet complete the remainder of the programme. We still had to sort out the key exchange, but, as it turned out, that was the least of our immediate problems. To say Shenavall was full is to convey little of the reality. Some youth branch of Her Majesty's Armed Services had decided to take over the premises. Our arrival prompted a myriad of heads to pop out of skylights, windows and doors and the seething body within had squashed its serpentine body into every nook and cranny. We shoe-horned the lads into a corner while Ron and I spent the night in the damp and draughty porch. I had never heard of Colin MacDonald at the time but I would have had every sympathy for him if his first night in his cottage was anything like mine.

In the night it rained. Rain in the Lake District is inconvenient. It makes the ground soggy and the rocks greasy. Rain in Scotland is dangerous. Between ourselves and our rendezvous was a river which flowed into Loch na Sealga. Yesterday's burbling burn was now a violent stampede. Ron tried to ford it but after only a couple of yards it had reached his thighs and was threatening to dash him off his feet. Plan B (or C or D depending which way you look at it) was called upon. We *could* work our way upstream until the flood became fordable, but there was no way of telling how long that would take and we would probably be in cloud and might well miss the other party. As this would have been somewhat inconvenient, we retreated once more to the Dundonnell Hotel to think again. Tiddly-winks was beginning to look quite a good option.

All this took place in the so-called summer of 1979

and by that time both Carnmore and Shenavall had been in the care of the Mountain Bothies Association for nearly fifteen years. Recreational bothying, as opposed to enforced stays on the hill as part of the job, really gained momentum after the Second World War. A growth in the economy and the flexibility offered by ex-army jeeps combined to relocate the inhabitants of the more remote areas into the towns and villages. As a result, many farms and crofts were abandoned, and as the workers departed, the ramblers moved in. But they were not alone. As with any deserted building, the fingers of decay also seize their chance. The wind first lifts a tile, inviting the rain to enter, then plaster peels, doors rot on their hinges and windows shrink within their frames. Many a property owner, once the first flush of pride in ownership has paled, all too well dreads the outcome of the battle between bricks and mortar and the forces of Nature.

Remarks appeared in bothy books lamenting the state of the fabric, accompanied by impassioned resolutions to do something about it and, as is usually the case, these discussions engendered more heat than light. But cometh the hour, cometh, in this case, Mr and Mrs Heath. In 1965 Bernard and Brenda rescued the house at Tunskeen in Galloway, then, encouraged by this success, inspired the formation of an Association 'to maintain simple shelters in remote country for the use and benefit of all who love the wild and lonely places'. This initial ambition spread its wings throughout the Highlands and such was the extent of the initial research that by 1971 Irvine Butterfield was able to produce a register of approximately 400 buildings that were potential bothy material.

As the project gained momentum, so did the organisation. A hierarchy of Bothy Maintenance Officers and Area Organisers emerged, overseen by a Director of Projects who generally steered the ship. Thereafter, the whole affair was sustained by volunteer labour and membership subscription. The enterprise was a triumph and by the end of the century the Mountain Bothies Association's 'portfolio' of bothy properties had topped 100 and Bernard and Brenda had been awarded the British Empire Medal for services to outdoor recreation.

The real strength of the Association lay within its philosophy—an open-door policy with no special privileges for members. There were no Youth Hostelish rules, each person helped according to his or her means and opportunities and, as outdoor organisations go, it was as utopian as could be hoped for. But society moves on and bureaucracy keeps pace and the earlier nautical metaphor proved not altogether inapt. Before the skipper and his crew, the reefs of litigation loomed. If a volunteer were to be injured during the course of mending a roof, could the Trustees, the other volunteers or even the membership itself be held legally responsible? Laws concerning Health & Safety and Child Welfare appeared on the statute books. Suddenly, the elementary precaution of safeguarding a simple shelter against the ravages of wind and rain became fraught with hidden forensic danger.

The Committee, however, seemed to take these matters in its stride, adjusting its response in a measured and considered manner. Yet there was one problem that seemed to exercise the mind more than most. Rats were inevitable but could be swept under the floorboards to be dealt with in due course. Humans were more of a problem and eventually, as the word of free, empty, dry spaces got round, impromptu ceilidhs turned into mini-raves, where fabric was torn from its fittings to feed the fire and litter and food remnants were left scattered around the site.

The immediate response of the majority of members was that all information should be withdrawn and the locations kept as secret as possible, but tardy shutting of the bothy door has the same result as with any other rural outbuilding. Much debate ensued and no doubt the wail went up 'if we could only restrict the use to the "right" sort of people', and there was even talk of the bothies being locked against general access. But after the immediate fuss, during which everything from the over-enthusiasm of outdoor writers to the current educational system was blamed, matters settled into a reasonable perspective. Only a few bothies were really at risk and usually the threat of closure did the trick.

Yet, whatever the difficulties, the pros always seem to outweigh the cons. Even a cursory inspection of the MBA's Journals and newsletters shows that people may have put a lot into but also taken a lot out of the various projects. Oddly enough, the success of the enterprise may partially have sprung from a reaction to the far greater vandalism of the 1950s and 60s. The urge to live in ugly chic had led to the ripping out of marble fireplaces and the destruction of tiled surfaces that would have long outlived their synthetic substitutes. Restoration became the rage, whether it was Tottering Towers or the humble croft, and to see a worthy example of the Association's contribution you need look no further than the rebuilding of Dibidil at the south end of Rum.

It all started in 1968 after a typical half-sun, half-mist day on the hill, when Sandy Cousins, Scottish mountaineer and writer, eased himself down the slopes of Sgurr nan Gillean and took in the scenery. Before starting the trudge back to Kinloch, he sat and smoked a meditative pipe and what occupied his thoughts were the ruins of an old croft and the possibility of restoring it into a bothy. The cottage had been built in 1849 and it was showing its age. Abandoned at the end of the nineteenth century, all that remained were the four ground-floor walls and gable ends, crowned, somewhat incongruously, by cracked chimney pots. Sandy tapped out his pipe and set off on the homeward path, marshalling his thoughts as how best to persuade the Nature Conservancy to let the recently formed MBA renovate the property.

Two years later, the job dropped on the plate of the Director of Projects with the remit to put together a team for the purpose. Irvine Butterfield was faced with various problems, ranging from lack of local knowledge to specialist help with building specs and nautical transportation. In far-off Yorkshire it seemed almost impossible but, to his surprise, offers flooded in, mainly through the good offices of Margaret Brown, the Association's rep in Glasgow, and the Royal Navy who offered the use of a Gemini

Inflatable and a posse of junior-ranking officers. It seemed the pipe-dream might become a reality.

It was decided the job should be split into two stages: Easter, when Bruce Watt's ferry would be available to transport the building materials and stand off Dibidil Bay while the Gemini ferried the cargo ashore; and a fortnight during the summer, when a construction party would gather to complete the job. Matters did not run smoothly. The roof sheeting had failed to arrive in Mallaig and with the 'Western Isles' having a limited window to make the voyage and the virtual impossibility of coordinating the volunteers for another weekend, matters looked as bad as they could get. After a legion of phone calls, the station master at Mallaig was able to pull rank over a sidings' clerk in Glasgow and everything arrived in the nick of time. All seemed well but, as so many bothy dwellers have found, the weather tends to have the final say and it was not in the dulcet tones of a gentle zephyr.

The forecast of Force 6, rising to Gale Force 9, was enough to persuade the skipper of the ferry that any unloading at the south of the island was out of the question, so he decided to discharge his cargo on the quayside at Kinloch. The building material had arrived in Rum but lay, a forlorn heap, at the wrong end of the island. The solution, which owed everything to the courage, determination and sheer physical effort shown by the Navy and employees of the Nature Conservancy, is faithfully described by Butterfield in his subsequent publication, *A Hebridean Adventure*. As is the rebuild, which took place in kinder weather (if heatwave, midgewave and tropical storms deserve that description) under the watchful eyes of Bill Mejury, the volunteer craftsman joiner, and the ubiquitous Bs. Thanks to the efforts of Roderick Manson, Butterfield's account has recently been reprinted, with additional memories of the Dibidil Reunions where details of somewhat violent games of football, evenings round the fire and the infamous 'Bevvy Run' are enthusiastically recalled.

If bivvies and bothies are all too spartan for your taste, there is the third choice. Rather better bed and breakfasts come at a price, but you receive in return a warm bed, drying facilities and food cooked by someone else. Although hotels and the like have obvious advantages, they do not leave the same impression as bivvies or bothies (maybe the provision of mattresses is a factor) and in this day of commercial conformity much of their individual flavour has been lost. No longer is the entrance hall of the inn at Wasdale thronged with the climbing impedimenta that distinguished the Abrahams' nineteenth-century picture postcard. Nor are ladies taking tea in the lounge likely to be disconcerted by the sound of an ivory spheroid crashing into the woodwork during a particularly lively tournament of billiard fives in the neighbouring smoke room. All has changed. The ornate dinner gongs of old no longer boom out their pre-prandial command.

But there was a time when the likes of the Wastwater Hotel, Pen y Gwryd and King's House, along with their more homely counterparts such as Mary Campbell's 'famous den' in Glen Brittle, were part of the weave of British climbing history and tradition. The reason is uncomplicated. When the sport began, transport was less reliable and popping up from London to Glencoe for a weekend was not really an option. This is not to suggest that the old-timers lacked get up and go. Dorothy Pilley, in her role as Secretary for the London Section of the Fell and Rock, reported that members (if they did not mind the indignity of travelling with the post) could get three days in the Lakes by catching the night mail. To take advantage of this cheap weekend return they had to leave Willesden Junction at one minute past midnight on Saturday morning and be back at Euston by 5 am on Tuesday. Given such an option, it

Iron Works, remarked, 'a hut was prob-
 a word for it.'[1]

ens, which included members of the
reagh Dhu, were superficially in broad
ith the principles of the MBA but had
adopt a rather different hospitality plan.
were allowed to enter might even be wel-
 information about plum routes waiting
ed, only to discover, on their return, that
d (like the supposed route) had mysteri-
peared. If anyone approached they didn't
ots simply threw stones at them until they
 But times have changed and it is now less
 the residents of the nearby King's House
rmed by violent arm-wrestling competi-
lood-curdling threats directed at passing
s. Perhaps the hotel's website tells the cur-
. On the 'How to Locate Us' page is the
 of directions regarding road and rail but
lso a paragraph entitled 'By Air', which
ou have a helicopter you can land just outside
door.

days, most of this way of life seems redun-
 ghosts of Herford and Kirkus would not
comfortably in what remains. The opportu-
 exploration are globally finite and the small

is not surprising the majority decided to make their
stay a longish one. As a result, certain hotels became
generally accepted as the places to meet, refresh
friendships and plan and record routes new and old.

Of the three areas already indicated, the Lake
District was probably the best served. Not only was
there an established tourist industry, but there was
also a greater number of climbing centres. The cliffs
that surrounded Wasdale, Buttermere, Langdale and
Coniston were quite separate, particularly when travelling by road, and soon advertisements for a variety
of hotels began to appear in the journals of the Fell
and Rock. Wasdale, with Scafell, Gable and the easiest access to Pillar, was always the favourite, but the
Sun Inn at Coniston had its fair number of devotees
and it was there that climbers from the Cumbrian
coast first mooted the idea of forming a Lake District
climbing club. But the days have gone since the cliffs
of Scafell dictated the hotel of choice. As the climbers
emerged from the recesses onto the smoother planes,
the emphasis shifted elsewhere. At the same time
came social change, where the new breed of working-
class climbers were more likely to be found brewing-
up in tents and adapted barns than loitering in the
Residents' Lounge, waiting for the gong to announce
their evening repast.

A similar pattern had emerged in North Wales. But unlike the Lakes, the accommodation around Capel Curig was sufficient to serve the compact area that contained the Welsh cliffs, so no constellation of climbing inns was created. Climbers would stay at the Pen y Gwryd and Pen y Pass Hotels but tended to socialise over port and brandy in, for many, the more convenient Home Counties. Eventually, the need for some sort of association arose and in May 1897 an informal dinner was planned at the Café Monico, where plans could be discussed and notes compared. The upshot was a decision to move their dinner meets to North Wales and form an 'English Climbing Club'. In 1898, in the Pen y Gwryd Hotel, the Climbers' Club was formed.

There seems no doubt that the club hoped to be regarded as some younger relative of the Alpine Club and many of its members belonged to both organisations. As a result, it tended to be over London-centric and, at times, particularly with regard to the publication of guidebooks for general use, appeared rather aloof, jealously protecting its cliffs against intruders. But rock climbing is the one activity where unjustified self-opinion can be most easily deflated, and overbearing conduct would provoke, first, dislike of and then indifference towards any self-appointed

guardian of British
detractors, the likes of
more amused than an
in *The Hard Years*, the
Oxbridge accents and i
along the lines of 'Rai
now, Cecil. Doo come

Scotland was a mixt
south of the Border. It h
mountainous areas were
be established, and the S
smoke-filled bar but in
ing circumstances of the C
Of those hotels that clim
the King's House at the he
ded in tradition, but whe
ing notoriety even those h
the knee to the noisy nei
Jacksonville, an early exar
prise, started life as a ruin
an ex-army tent. But, by dir
timber and corrugated iron,
to the state where Jeff Con
John Cunningham, could
palatial. American visitors w
Chouinard, ice gear innovat

Great Pacific
ably too kin
Its deniz
legendary C
sympathy w
decided to
Those who
comed with
to be climb
all their fo
ously disap
like, the Sc
went away
likely that
will be al
tions or
Sassenach
rent story
usual typ
there is
reads: *If*
the front
Nowa
dant. Th
have sat
nities fo

stock of British cliffs was bound to run out sooner rather than later. By the mid 1970s, all that was left were scraps. Standards continued to rise, but if the only ambition is gymnastic excellence, it might as well happen in the warmth of a leisure centre as on a windswept gritstone edge. Today, serious climbers, after a brief apprenticeship on local rock, look, as did the Victorian pioneers, outside these shores for their greater achievements.

All that will be left of what once had been are fading photographs and half-remembered myths. Unless, of course, the uncontrolled pursuit of Mammon causes economic collapse and those looking for adventure have to fall back on their own resources, sheltering under local boulders and makeshift howffs. Perhaps the day will come when a group gets together to restore the ruin of what was clearly once a large and sumptuous residence and, when searching the cellar, wonder what possible use the former occupants could have found for a rather over-elaborate gong.

Ends

Old climbers never die, they simply hit the grit. No doubt the appropriate department of the car sticker industry has realised that a generation born around the Second World War is now approaching its dotage. Sustained by free milk, cod liver oil and full employment, the ranks of UK climbers were swelled by a classless gathering whose ambition lay beyond the easily accessible local crags. Unemployment between the wars had already prised the sport out of the fingers of the well-heeled, with a consequent rise in standard, but in the 1950s and 60s such was the general popularity of moving safely in danger-ous places that the leading proponents approached the status of household names. As with all such, their obituaries are probably already on file.

Assuming there is no volte-face in Britain's inter-pretation of European Directive No 2001/45 (Tem-porary Work at Height) [as amended by Annex 11 to the 1989 Directive] which could, given over-zealous application by Health and Safety officials, result in rock climbing being banned altogether, there are a number of ways in which your climbing days can be numbered. In theory, you can continue in some form is not surprising the majority decided to make their stay a longish one. As a result, certain hotels became generally accepted as the places to meet, refresh friendships and plan and record routes new and old.

Of the three areas already indicated, the Lake District was probably the best served. Not only was there an established tourist industry, but there was also a greater number of climbing centres. The cliffs that surrounded Wasdale, Buttermere, Langdale and Coniston were quite separate, particularly when travelling by road, and soon advertisements for a variety of hotels began to appear in the journals of the Fell and Rock. Wasdale, with Scafell, Gable and the easiest access to Pillar, was always the favourite, but the Sun Inn at Coniston had its fair number of devotees and it was there that climbers from the Cumbrian coast first mooted the idea of forming a Lake District climbing club. But the days have gone since the cliffs of Scafell dictated the hotel of choice. As the climbers emerged from the recesses onto the smoother planes, the emphasis shifted elsewhere. At the same time came social change, where the new breed of working-class climbers were more likely to be found brewing-up in tents and adapted barns than loitering in the Residents' Lounge, waiting for the gong to announce their evening repast.

A similar pattern had emerged in North Wales. But unlike the Lakes, the accommodation around Capel Curig was sufficient to serve the compact area that contained the Welsh cliffs, so no constellation of climbing inns was created. Climbers would stay at the Pen y Gwryd and Pen y Pass Hotels but tended to socialise over port and brandy in, for many, the more convenient Home Counties. Eventually, the need for some sort of association arose and in May 1897 an informal dinner was planned at the Café Monico, where plans could be discussed and notes compared. The upshot was a decision to move their dinner meets to North Wales and form an 'English Climbing Club'. In 1898, in the Pen y Gwryd Hotel, the Climbers' Club was formed.

There seems no doubt that the club hoped to be regarded as some younger relative of the Alpine Club and many of its members belonged to both organisations. As a result, it tended to be over London-centric and, at times, particularly with regard to the publication of guidebooks for general use, appeared rather aloof, jealously protecting its cliffs against intruders. But rock climbing is the one activity where unjustified self-opinion can be most easily deflated, and overbearing conduct would provoke, first, dislike of and then indifference towards any self-appointed guardian of British climbing values. Among the detractors, the likes of the Rock and Ice were probably more amused than annoyed. As Joe Brown explains in *The Hard Years*, their response was to adopt faux Oxbridge accents and issue their climbing commands along the lines of 'Raighto, I've got a bloody belay now, Cecil. Doo come yup.'

Scotland was a mixture of the climbing elements south of the Border. It had its climbing hotels but the mountainous areas were too far spread for a coterie to be established, and the SMC was born not in some smoke-filled bar but in the somewhat more uplifting circumstances of the Glasgow Christian Institute. Of those hotels that climbers most frequently used, the King's House at the head of Glencoe was embedded in tradition, but when it came to mountaineering notoriety even those hallowed halls had to bend the knee to the noisy neighbours across the road. Jacksonville, an early example of self-build enterprise, started life as a ruined sheepfank covered by an ex-army tent. But, by dint of additional masonry, timber and corrugated iron, it was illicitly developed to the state where Jeff Connor, in his biography of John Cunningham, could describe it as relatively palatial. American visitors were less impressed. Yvon Chouinard, ice gear innovator and founder of the

Great Pacific Iron Works, remarked, 'a hut was probably too kind a word for it.'[1]

Its denizens, which included members of the legendary Creagh Dhu, were superficially in broad sympathy with the principles of the MBA but had decided to adopt a rather different hospitality plan. Those who were allowed to enter might even be welcomed with information about plum routes waiting to be climbed, only to discover, on their return, that all their food (like the supposed route) had mysteriously disappeared. If anyone approached they didn't like, the Scots simply threw stones at them until they went away. But times have changed and it is now less likely that the residents of the nearby King's House will be alarmed by violent arm-wrestling competitions or blood-curdling threats directed at passing Sassenachs. Perhaps the hotel's website tells the current story. On the 'How to Locate Us' page is the usual type of directions regarding road and rail but there is also a paragraph entitled 'By Air', which reads: *If you have a helicopter you can land just outside the front door.*

Nowadays, most of this way of life seems redundant. The ghosts of Herford and Kirkus would not have sat comfortably in what remains. The opportunities for exploration are globally finite and the small stock of British cliffs was bound to run out sooner rather than later. By the mid 1970s, all that was left were scraps. Standards continued to rise, but if the only ambition is gymnastic excellence, it might as well happen in the warmth of a leisure centre as on a windswept gritstone edge. Today, serious climbers, after a brief apprenticeship on local rock, look, as did the Victorian pioneers, outside these shores for their greater achievements.

All that will be left of what once had been are fading photographs and half-remembered myths. Unless, of course, the uncontrolled pursuit of Mammon causes economic collapse and those looking for adventure have to fall back on their own resources, sheltering under local boulders and makeshift howffs. Perhaps the day will come when a group gets together to restore the ruin of what was clearly once a large and sumptuous residence and, when searching the cellar, wonder what possible use the former occupants could have found for a rather over-elaborate gong.

Ends

Old climbers never die, they simply hit the grit. No doubt the appropriate department of the car sticker industry has realised that a generation born around the Second World War is now approaching its dotage. Sustained by free milk, cod liver oil and full employment, the ranks of UK climbers were swelled by a classless gathering whose ambition lay beyond the easily accessible local crags. Unemployment between the wars had already prised the sport out of the fingers of the well-heeled, with a consequent rise in standard, but in the 1950s and 60s such was the general popularity of moving safely in danger-ous places that the leading proponents approached the status of household names. As with all such, their obituaries are probably already on file.

Assuming there is no volte-face in Britain's inter-pretation of European Directive No 2001/45 (Tem-porary Work at Height) [as amended by Annex 11 to the 1989 Directive] which could, given over-zealous application by Health and Safety officials, result in rock climbing being banned altogether, there are a number of ways in which your climbing days can be numbered. In theory, you can continue in some form or another for as long as you please. There is usually no moment, no epiphany when you realise that you should have devoted your life to basket-weaving or politics. Yet, as circumstance inevitably shapes events, so do events shape circumstance and if I look back on the events that eventually consigned my karabiners to the loft or, at least, as appendages to a grandchild's swing, I can recall two moments when the compass needle swung from its intended direction.

The circumstances that led to the first event happened on a pleasant enough day. There was not a real or metaphorical cloud in the sky. The route was not long and the rock was solid with good holds and, although such struggle as I had seemed to last an age, it was but a microsecond when compared to the hours of agony that others have endured. It all happened on a curiously constructed climb, the main thrust of which was an undercut buttress poised above a triangular bay of very steep grass. As, at the time, it was thought that a direct ascent via the overhang was not possible, the recommended approach traversed up and across a subsidiary face that was set at right angles to the desired objective. The two pieces of rock resembled an open book (as it turned out, anything but to me) with a shallow crack running up its interior spine. It was at the base of this you placed such protection that you owned, which in our case wasn't very much. The solution to the problem, for it was no more than that, was straightforward. You made what progress you could up the crack until it was eventually possible to reach out to your left, where a good hold allowed you to transfer to the main buttress before pulling over the bulge onto easier rock.

I climbed the crack until the good hold was just within reach. It was then I made the two types of mistake that always betray a novice. First, rather than make a further and more difficult move up the crack, which would have eased the transfer considerably as my weight would have been better distributed, I half abandoned the crack once my fingers were touching the hold, with the intention of manhandling myself over the bulge. Second, I dithered, thus losing any momentum that the original move might have created. It soon became clear, after one or two rather ineffective, or for that matter ineffectual, attempts, that I no longer had sufficient strength to overcome the friction created by the bulge and lodge myself on the available foothold. In between these efforts, I tried to return to the crack but, unwilling to relinquish my one sure point of contact, did little but expend what remaining energy I had. Eventually, spread-eagled between a Scylla and Charybdis of my own making and unable to hang on any longer, I had no alternative but to attempt to reverse the original move or fall off. What followed was sequentially simple. I let go of the hold. My foot slipped from the crack. I fell off. My only thought as I flew through the air was, 'Ah well, at least that's over!'

But, as with small children and drunks, there is a providence that befriends the inept. The unintended but fortunate result of these acrobatics meant that instead of swinging with a crash onto the subsidiary rock face, I landed on the crown of the steep grassy bay. At this point I bounced, performing what felt like a somersault and half twist to land in an elasticated heap at the exact moment the solitary runner came into play. It was probably quite spectacular to observe, the sort of thing that people pay good money for, but, in fact, it was little more than a convincing vindication of the principles of mechanics and Newton's various Laws of Motion. My Second, having observed all this tomfoolery for several minutes, was understandably anxious as to the outcome. We were due to depart for a fortnight in Skye the following day and he had paid in advance for his travel and accommodation.

This did not signal the end of my climbing ambition, but it acted as one of those checks and balances that enable us to tunnel a way through life and, as I continued to climb for several more decades, it did not even signify the beginning of the end. It was, however, the end of the beginning. Up to that point in life I had decided that if I put my mind to it, I could make a reasonable success of anything I chose to do. Thus, I had dutifully followed the rules (and graded lists) in the approved manner on the assumption that I would eventually finish somewhere near the top of the table.

This particular Fall from Grace altered matters. As I watched my companion solo with comparative ease across the rock to retrieve the gear, I realised that, unlike most activities where you can smudge the edges of success and failure, climbing was different. You were either on or you were off and there were no nearly or almost. I was still ambitious, compiling the perennial hit-list, but one thing was clear. Another Joe of any hue I was not, nor was meant to be. But the mind is capable of its own contortions. Perceptions shift and alternative targets start to harden on the horizon. Targets which could be adjusted to suit circumstances. So it was not long before I was able to plant my flag on the moral high ground by deciding that what real climbing was really about was quality rather than mere difficulty.

Time passed once more, now measured in years rather than minutes, and the climbs gradually became fewer and less frequent. Like most people who take up the sport, my eventual demise lacked any momentous explosion. It is also true to say that it ended not as a whimper but rather as a long exhalation of resigned acceptance. The end, or at least the beginning of this end, of my climbing days came after an occasion that, although serious enough, seemed at the time to be relatively incidental.

I had some years previously moved to Macclesfield and had been delighted to discover that a new series of Peak District guidebooks was beginning to emerge. They were produced for and by the Peak Committee of the British Mountaineering Council and Volume 1 was entitled *The Sheffield-Stanage Area*. This was on the wrong side of the Peak from our point of view and, although we were well enough acquainted with the various sections of Stanage, it was not over-tempting to exchange the nearby Roaches for foreign fields, even if they did have such intriguing names as Bell Hagg and Agden Rocher. Nevertheless, we felt that sometime in an uncertain future we should make at least one visit to Wharncliffe Crags, for, according to the guidebook, this was the birthplace of gritstone climbing. Despite the self-publicity of Professor E A

Baker, whose outpourings such as *Moor, Crags and Caves of the High Peak* gave the impression that it was he who had principally instigated and developed climbing in the Peak, the early exploration throughout the district had been made by J W Puttrell who, with his fellow silversmith W J Watson, had, according to our new guidebook, 'turned Wharncliffe into a veritable gymnasium'.[1]

As it happened, some years were to pass before Phil and I started at the Deepcar end of the crags and began to work our way towards Wharncliffe Lodge. The idea was to do any climb that caught our eye, as well as paying historical homage to our gritstone forebears. These included a variety of cracks by Puttrell, Watson and Scarlett. We assumed that the last was the famed Harry of that ilk but, given that Hamlet appeared to be responsible for a nearby climb, I can't vouch for the historical authenticity of the Dramatis Personae. Nevertheless, to be on the safe side, we pressed the flesh on any titular Crack or Slab. We even did Byne's Route as a nod of recognition towards the General Editor whose guidebook we held in our hand.

To be honest, I did not think a great deal of the crag as Gritstone's Garden of Eden. On the day, the cracks were dank, without much sign of passage, and because the rock comes at the Coal Measure end of the sandstone spectrum it had a somewhat scruffy air. We were about to call it a day when the guidebook played its final card:

PUTTRELL AND
WATSON'S ROUTE   30 feet   *Very Difficult*
The climb looked even less prepossessing than the others. But, two for the price of one *and,* as added incentive for the upwardly mobile historian, the route description included an addendum that 'the layback is believed to be the first of its type to be done in the Peak District being of around 1889 vintage'.[1] That's settled then. Pop up this—homage done—down to the pub.

With a moment's thought, it could all have turned out very differently. We had already done routes by the two pioneers and even added a Puttrellian Progress for good measure. It certainly wasn't the first layback in recorded history. Haskett Smith probably did little else on his days off and, anyway, the term wasn't even invented until the 1920s and, moreover, as an trans-atlantic neologism by Rice Kemper Evans, the then American Vice-Consul at Sheffield. Not only didn't it look much of a climb, but the ground beneath it was covered in awkward blocks of rock under rank vegetation. On top of all that, it was beginning to rain. The obvious choice was to call it a day. As it turned out, 'choice' was the undoing, for at the top of the layback crack the route, according to what by now had become Holy Writ, went either to the left or right. The key to a successful layback is to keep moving, but at the top Phil stopped to weigh up the options. In this moment of indecision, his foot slipped and he fell the twelve feet to the ground. Nine hundred and ninety-nine times out of a thousand, it would have been no worse than a sprained ankle. In all similar circumstances on that particular day I would have been directly below his line of fall and the worst that would have happened would have been a tangle of undignified limbs. But, to find more even ground and also to improve my sightline as to which finish looked the better, I had moved some ten yards back from the foot of the cliff.

Even from that distance I could see the outcome of impact did not look promising. At the instant his body twisted to the ground, Phil's foot must have become trapped between two boulders. I had never realised how dislocated a dislocation could be. The only thing that appeared to connect his foot to his leg was his sock. It was one of those moments when you know you should do something immediately but you're not sure what. All I could think of was, 'Do you fancy a fag?' to a man who had just exerted a considerable amount of willpower in giving up smoking. The response was slightly strained: 'No, I think you'd better get help.'

The paralysis left and I scrabbled up to the top of the edge and set off in search of a phone. I probably went in the wrong direction for it seemed more than a long time before I eventually saw a house with telegraph poles leading towards it. I banged on the door. There was an anxious moment until someone eventually answered. All this might have contributed to my apparent state of exhausted shock when I asked if I could use his phone but it could not have explained the inventive ingenuity of a reporter from the local newspaper whose later account of my life-or-death dash across the 'inhospitable Yorkshire moorland' made the marathon efforts of Pheidippides seem little more than an evening stroll.

Eventually, an ambulance built more for comfort than speed and driven by a man of similar disposition, wheezed up. The apparent equipment on offer was a stretcher plus the sort of knapsack you sling across the body and over one shoulder, which looked as if it might contain little more than a couple of triangular bandages and a thermos flask. By this time I had got my bearings and set off up the hillside, making a beeline for the crag. After twenty yards, the ambulance man stopped and handed over the stretcher. A further twenty and the knapsack changed hands. Our progress was then punctuated by further pauses as various items of clothing were removed and I began to suspect that before we got to the victim, I might resemble a cricket umpire in a heatwave. The crag was eventually reached and, although Phil was made as comfortable as possible, it didn't seem to me that we were much further forward. Somehow we had to get him back to the ambulance across the same terrain that had caused more than enough problems unburdened.

Then it happened. It was a bit like that scene in *Zulu* when Michael Caine or someone offers his opinion that nothing much seems to be happening and, as if on cue, several thousand of the local populace appear on the skyline in a distinctly threatening manner. The fire brigade had arrived in force and their leader, flanked by his trusty crew, stood above us peering over the edge. I was about to explain when the said leader (I assume he was the leader as he wore a red helmet whereas the others wore yellow) issued a series of commands and suddenly ropes and attached equipment were flying in all directions. I offered a suggestion that if the aim was to get the injured to the top of the crag, there was a perfectly feasible path up which the stretcher could be carried, but clearly mountain rescue was part of their brief and mountain rescue they intended to do.

The stretcher with body was duly hauled up the cliff face while I walked round by the path to join them. The ambulance man retrieved his knapsack and sloped off home for his tea. The area at the top of the crag was bordered by a drystone wall and behind that, as it transpired, lay a road harbouring the fire engine and another ambulance. The wall had not only been too high for me to see over and choose a simpler route for my 'mercy dash', but was also too high for the stretcher to be transferred to the other side with any degree of security. The leader measured up the problem, then, with one of those flourishes favoured by the more sadistic type of Roman Emperor when despatching superfluous gladiators, gave the order. The top portion of a rampart which had been built with skilled hands and for centuries withstood the worst that northern weather could throw at it was demolished within seconds.

With the body stowed by a more streamlined crew, the brigade leapt aboard and, klaxon sounding, screeched off into the middle distance. Such was the splendour of this new conveyance and the marvel of its equipment that I began to wonder whether the first Good Samaritan had, in fact, been the genuine article. I suppose it was possible there existed a band of DIY first-aiders who happened to have acquired a decommissioned ambulance. Under the circumstances I never thought of asking about ID. But all were gone and only I and the gathering gloom were left, trying to recall where Phil had parked his car.

This did not mean I gave up climbing as a result. In fact, en route to and from hospital-visiting in Sheffield, I did a number of routes on the aforementioned Bell Hagg and Agden Rocher. But it did lead me to reappraise the situation. I had only climbed to any extent with two people—Phil and my wife. He was now *hors de combat* and it quickly emerged that this was not just a temporary inconvenience, but a serious setback. His ankle had been broken in a number of places and it took more than several months and a bone transplant before he was able to walk properly. All parties involved, not least his surgeon, insisted that he never set foot on steep rock again. The patient accepted his lot quite stoically and, having promised to restrict his mountain experience to plodding up hillsides, spent his spare time in the Himalayas. My wife now owned one and a bit children and, understandably, her priorities had begun to change.

So what had once been a ruling passion, the deciding factor for every holiday venue and weekend outing, began to wane. I still climbed regularly but most often by myself and closer to home. There were bursts of enthusiasm—a plan to complete a route on every substantial Scottish cliff springs to mind—but before I knew where I was, I was plodding up Munros, not really bagging them of course, just getting to know the Highlands rather than scraping at the surface. Then it was a case of: as I've done so many, I may as well do the lot; and from there it was only a step before buying books on Corbetts and Grahams and blaming my ineptitude (for the child is the father of the man) on the recalcitrance of various arthritic joints.

Why I Read...

... books on mountaineering. Not only read but also, in a rather desultory way, collect. Although a glance at the bookshelves would suggest that my selection, ranging from the Pamirs to Patagonia, is rather eclectic, closer examination will reveal that a significant number are books on climbing in Britain. And in this preponderance may well lie the answer to the question in the title. When I first started climbing, it was an age when currency restrictions, economic restraint and a degree of xenophobic timidity limited me and, I suspect, many others to holidays at home. You could read about the said Pams and Pats but in reality they were no more accessible than the fantasies of H G Wells or the celluloid revelations gleaned from *Aliens from Outer Space* showing at your local Odeon. Unless you had the ear of John Hunt or knew the right sort of string-puller, climbing on rock or ice in the 1950s meant, for a sizeable majority, climbing in Britain. It also meant that I needed information on British climbing and in those days, 'information' meant books.

I have already pointed out that, as part of the aforementioned economic restraint (a hardback novel could be ninety times more expensive than a newspaper), there was a seeming reluctance to publish mountaineering books on any subject other than British paramilitary success in the Himalayas and analagous examples of post-colonial angst. The climbing clubs seemed to have been similarly affected and most guidebooks were either out of print or not easily available. I have discussed the reasons for this elsewhere and there seems little point in going over old ground. Suffice to add that the outcome was a scavenging of second-hand bookshops and purchasing what I thought might be relevant to my immediate requirements, i.e. details of climbs in Britain. So I became the rather proud possessor of such literary giants as *Crag and Hound in Lakeland* by Claude E Benson and *Climbs in Cleveland* by no one in particular, rather than the more prominently displayed *Scrambles amongst the Alps*, a title which, along with the name of author, seemed to imply a content far too namby-pamby for my vaulting ambition.

During my borrowing and re-borrowing of the likes of *Mountaineering in Britain*, I noticed a narrative emerging. In it, climbing appeared to be as much a story as a sport. A record of heroes and villains, moral dilemmas and epic struggles. As always, the voice of history offered its asides and one of these retrospects emanated from the throat of an eminent Victorian Alpinist who pronounced that, whereas climbing in the Caucasus and the Alps was usually safe and rarely difficult, climbs in the English Lake District were both difficult and dangerous.

I was triumphant. Not only was my favouring of British climbs founded on a sound pragmatic base, but it was also wreathed in the qualities on which empires are founded. Clearly I had been right to ignore the continental baubles and spend my energy and resources on books concerning Britain and British climbing. Moreover, I felt entirely vindicated that I had decided to stick to climbing in Britain. This feeling was reinforced when, in the course of my researches, I discovered a dramatic account of Eagle's Nest Direct, at the time the pinnacle of my hopes. It had been first climbed by Godfrey Solly, one time Mayor of Birkenhead, my very own birthplace. The die, so to speak, were cast and the search for accounts of domestic activity intensified. Yet all this might explain why I read and collected but not necessarily why I read books on mountaineering.

The last sentence is interesting. Although there is no doubt about the meaning of the word 'read' when it is spoken aloud, it could on the page be interpreted variously. 'I read (red)' could mean that I used to read and no longer do, whereas 'I read (reed)' implies that I still do. Within this linguistic confusion may lie the answer to the question *why?* At the very least, I realised, when tackling the question, I should bear in mind the reason I read and collected in the past is not necessarily the same as the reason I read and collect now.

Another piece of the jigsaw is the odd coincidence that, at the time when I started taking a serious interest in climbing, I also stumbled across *The Waste Land*. An experience which I found singularly annoying. For the first time in my life (or so I fondly imagined) I had discovered a piece of writing in English that I didn't understand. I comprehended, by and large, the meaning of the words and had enough of a Classical education to pick up on the myths and have a stab at translating the tricky bits. But the problem was that it made no sense or, more accurately (as I later patiently explained to similar struggles from a lofty pedagogic height), it made no sense to me. In desperation I bought a Penguin publication entitled *Selected Prose* by T S Eliot in the hope of enlightenment. Not surprisingly, utter darkness ensued, but there was one essay that I found of interest.

In 'Tradition and the Individual Talent', it seemed to me Eliot was suggesting that, for any individual achievement to have worth, it should be rooted in and then grow out of its own tradition. He was talking particularly about poetry and the part that literary history and especially the output of its giants played in the advancement of any aspiring poet. Although my idea was rather fanciful, I came to think the same applied to climbing. Only by assimilating the history of climbing and the way in which it developed could the individual be said to be a climber and clamber, so to speak, onto the rack and pinion of mountaineering progress. Of course, the assertion would not have borne close examination but there was enough superficial evidence for it to fall in with my fledgling thoughts. Climbing, with its incremental grading system, encourages the idea of progression built on previous achievements and there were benchmark routes like Central Buttress on Scafell, Great Slab on Clogwyn Du'r Arddu and Cenotaph Corner on Clogwyn y Grochan, each of which, in the words of the now infallible Clark & Pyatt, 'marked not only the end of an era but also the beginning of a fresh and more exciting one'.[1]

In addition to supporting my half-baked theory, the much-borrowed *Mountaineering in Britain* had two further advantages. The first was a bibliography of every book that had been written on climbing in

Britain and this was sufficiently short to encourage reading and, when possible, collecting the lot. The second was a listed explanation of the superscripted figures that littered the text. Naturally some of these related to the books contained in the bibliography, but, more interestingly, there were a number of references to the Journals of the Scottish Mountaineering Club, the Climbers' Club and the Fell and Rock. These all appeared fertile ground in which to find further information but it was to the last that I was immediately attracted.

The seeds of this fascination had been planted many years before. Although I had not appreciated it at the time, I now realise that I was fortunate to have a father who saw holidays not as a necessity for idling the time on ice cream and donkey rides, but as an opportunity to gain what would today be described as a holistic experience of the area visited. Among the welter of cathedrals, dreaming spires and Stratford theatricals appeared a holiday in the Lake District and the experience had a profound effect on how I was to spend the rest of my life. Because of the geographical juxtaposition of Sunderland and Ullswater, it was decided the easiest and probably cheapest mode of transport was a taxi cab. This, in itself, was a glamorous enough start, but the subsequent combination of boating on the lake, climbing the fells, including a 'scramble' along Striding Edge, and watching the wrestling and hound trail at Grasmere Sports more than offset the obligatory visit to Wordsworth's Cottage.

So, to discover that there were publications that covered both my favoured area of England and a history of climbing in the district seemed too good to be true and I set out to read and ideally own the complete run of FRCC Journals from the Club's inception to the present day. I was delighted to find the consequent reading lent even greater weight to my 'Tradition' theory. The volumes contained first-hand accounts of famous climbs and the section entitled 'Climbs, Old and New' showed how the ladder of progress had been erected and followed.

With due respect, I climbed the rungs. The Victorians caused little problem, though I can't say that I followed the time-honoured practice of combating the practical problems of snow and hail by climbing in stockinged feet. After which, with a few judiciously avoided exceptions, the first half of the twentieth century didn't go too badly either. Then the head hit a glass ceiling. Not an inapt metaphor, as I could see clearly enough the continuing staircase and with it the potential rise of this particular 'Individual

Talent', but it was not to be. Suicide Wall, Cemetery Gates and Sepulchre said it all.

The result of this train of events was a shift in emphasis in my choice of required reading. I continued to pay homage to the much appreciated topographical information that the Journals provided (for what other possible reason do I number Pedagogues' Chimney on Striddle Crag among my mountaineering achievements?) but, equally, I began to appreciate that there were other elements at work. In addition to the contributions by such luminaries as Haskett Smith, I discovered the likes of 'Charlie' Holland, Mabel Barker and Geoffrey Sutton, who may well have revealed relevant information on the nature of particular climbs but, in their considered musings, could more interestingly tell a tale and turn a phrase. I began to realise that climbing literature was considerably more than a list of achievements and that Bentley Beetham's 'Billiard Fives', his essay on the idiosyncratic arrangements for home entertainment at the Wasdale Head Hotel, was just as important as his 'Shepherds Crag Reports a Dividend', an essay describing the climbs he had unearthed on the vegetated crags that flank Derwentwater.

Consequently, I revisited books I had read years before, only to discover that among the writings of, for instance, W H Murray there were several chapters that I had skimmed and dismissed as they didn't contain useful information on Glencoe, Skye or the Ben. Whereas, once, in my imagination I had swung across his improbable overhangs and effortlessly balanced on holdless slabs, I now began to enjoy his descriptions of the crossing of Rannoch Moor and a storm on Liathach.

As a result, I was suddenly back where I started, buying any second-hand book with a title that seemed vaguely relevant to my new enthusiasm. There can't be many readers that have Molly Lefebure's *Scratch and Co: the great cat expedition* and Sir Arnold Lunn's *The Englishman in the Alps, being a collection of English prose and poetry relating to the Alps* as neighbours on their bookshelf. Nothing escaped consideration. Even the detective yarns of Glyn Carr, despite the red herrings appearing as bearded taciturns fond of long, solitary walks, had a certain appeal. Although no longer a great admirer of the genre (I had, in my youth, rather surfeited on a diet of pipe-smoking private eyes and gumshoes masquerading as Roman Catholic priests), there was a reason to make the deductive cogitations of Sir Abercrombie Lewker an exception. The denouement was invariably set in the hills of North Wales. To fully appreciate and anticipate the outcome, it was a great help if you understood the rock-climbing intricacies of the ridges of Tryfan or why it might take as long as it did to cover the rough ground between the PYG and the Devil's Kitchen.

Further reading reinforced the belief that the canvas was much wider than I had imagined and then, by happy coincidence, as if in compensation for all the years of literary famine, established classics began to be reprinted. Alistair Borthwick's *Always a Little Further* and Oppenheimer's *The Heart of Lakeland* became immediately and cheaply accessible. Soon after, publishers like Diadem and Ernest Press started to encourage an interest in the mountain literature of the past as well as championing new endeavours. The latter in particular promoted authors who wished to undertake original research into great events of climbing history. Books appeared on Edwards, Herford, Kirkus, and the inner politics of Scottish climbing were revealed by the likes of *May the fire be always lit* and *Creagh Dhu Climber*. Out of the tragedy that surrounded the deaths of Pete Boardman and Joe Tasker grew a literary prize, named in their remembrance, that encouraged new writers to express their views and recall their experiences. Suddenly every corner of the British climbing scene seemed to be lit by new evidence and fresh insight.

By now, I started to view books on mountaineering as I view tourist guides to foreign lands: they may well be a useful introduction to the subject but are usually a better read after you have been there. They seemed to make more sense and certainly appeared more interesting when I knew what the authors were on about and could share and compare their reactions with my own. So, as my own experience increased, so did the field widen. But of more importance, I quickly realised that climbing experiences are universal and the feelings on successfully completing a climb were the same whether in the Dolomites or the Lake District. This, of course, loosened the strings of the xenophobic corset to a considerable extent and opened up a new field of interest.

It was only then I fully realised the variety that was on offer. Books for all seasons seemed to move through the full register: the comic (*The Ridiculous Mountains*), the sardonic (*One Man's Mountains*), the satiric (*The Ascent Of Rum Doodle*), the tragic (*The White Spider*), the philosophic (*Thoughts of a Mountaineer*), the historic (*High Peak*), the biographic (*Menlove*), the sociological (*One Green Bottle*), the empathic (*Let's Go Climbing*), the epic (*Touching the Void*), the inspirational (*On the Heights*), the reflective (*Climbing Days*) and the simply homely (*In Mountain Lakeland*).

This list is more or less off the top of my head and the examples are the first to spring to mind, with alternatives easily found. It was while compiling it that I was reminded of a somewhat more measured test that forms the basis for a chapter in *Undiscovered Scotland*. MacAlpine, the author's brother-in-law, accuses Murray of gilding the lily or, at best, being carefully selective when it comes to writing up his climbing experiences. To settle the argument, MacAlpine suggests Murray should produce his diaries, 'take three lucky dips—then publish the results if you dare'.[2]

This in turn reminded me that I have long held and, on occasion, voiced the opinion that climbing literature has produced finer writing than any other sporting pastime, so I decided to put the theory to the test. I asked an impartial witness to select three books from my choice of twenty (to give my theory a chance) whereafter I opened each at random in the hopes of finding on the chosen page a sentence or two that neatly and memorably encapsulated some aspect of climbing. To be fair to the authors I give briefly the context. This is what came up.

Tom Patey describes an abseiling incident during the first winter traverse of the Cuillin Ridge:

This would have been all right if it had not been for three significant factors. The rope had reached him at a slight angle; the slope fell away at a slight angle; and he was wearing crampons.[3]

Bill Murray reaches the end of a tumultuous day on Liathach:

So we stripped to the skin in the wind and darkness, then dived inside to pull on dry sweaters and sleeping bags. We heard the music of a purring primus, watched pure snow change in the pot to grey slush, then to bubbling clarity ...[2]

Jim Perrin looks back on 'the land that time forgot':

I don't know why this should be, but the general run of cliffs around Ogwen are very clean. There are some which are not, of course—Gallt yr Ogof or Clogwyn y Geifr are as dirty as any pioneer could wish—but most of them are quite sparkling.[4]

So, as the man said, 'these fragments I have shored against my ruins'. Or, to avoid trespassing once more over Mr Eliot's waste land, I could perhaps stick to safer Shavian territory and suggest as an answer to my original question—those who can still climb, do, those who can't, read.